DEDICATED
TO

Purple Deserts

Walking in Stardust

and

Polar Bears in Denver

ACKNOWLEDGEMENTS

We give special thanks to the following people without whose work this book would not have been possible: Richard Bandler, John Grinder, Leslie Cameron-Bandler, Judith DeLozier, Robert Dilts, David Gordon, Maribeth Meyers-Anderson, Stephen Lankton, and the late Milton H. Erickson, M.D.

We would also like to extend our appreciation to the following individuals who supported us in this endeavour: Susan L. Edwards, Sandy Anderson, Bruce Douglass, M. Diane Vincent, Jeanette Bowman, Karen Bos, Wanda Daniels, Bill Maine, Victor Roberge, Hank Sundell, Linnaea Marvel-Mell, Nicola Malatesta, Debbie Zieminski, Carmen Hall, Terry Boortz, Angela Daniels, and our parents.

TABLE OF CONTENTS

INTRODUCTION

During the mid 1970's, Richard Bandler, John Grinder and their associates began an investigation into the process of communication and change which later became known as NeuroLinguistic Programming (N.L.P.). This process model of communication had its foundation firmly rooted in linguistics, neuropsychology and cybernetics. Mr. Bandler, a mathematician, and Dr. Grinder, a linguist, set out on a quest to better understand how people change. In the ten or so years that have passed since this new field began, numerous books have been published on various aspects and applications of N.L.P. The purpose of our book is to offer a systematic explanation of the basic principles of N.L.P. as they apply to psychotherapy and to make them available to any therapist who wishes to increase his/her own options in working with clients. We are very much indebted to Mr. Bandler and Dr. Grinder for their wonderful insights which have greatly enriched the practice of psychotherapy. We bid you, the reader, to sit back, relax and allow yourself to join us on a unique journey.

Kim M. Kostere
Linda K. Malatesta
Bloomfield Hills, Michigan
August, 1984

PART I

*The known is finite, the unknown infinite;
intellectually we stand on an islet in the midst of
an illimitable ocean of inexplicability. Our business
in every generation is to reclaim a little more land.*

T. H. Huxley

1

SCIENCE AND MODELING

Since the time of the early Greek and Roman philosophers, we as a species have taken knowledge and categorized it. Initially, most knowledge was encompassed in the field called "philosophy". The philosophers drew the bulk of their information from introspection, relying little upon empiricism. Long days and nights were spent in ancient times, by the great philosophers, discussing such areas as Epistemology, Metaphysics and Psychology. As time went on, these learned men and women began to focus their attention outward, paying more attention to actual events taking place in the cosmos around them. Instead of using introspection to build theories, observation took over as the primary tool for gathering information and hence science was born. Many of the modern sciences, such as physics, astronomy, chemistry, and biology arose from these observations, and along with them the scientific method.

During the times of Isaac Newton, the goals of science were to discover and understand the laws of nature as they occurred in the universe, independent of any possible influence of the scientist. In this scientific model it was thought that cause and effect relationships occurred and could be <u>known</u> without the need to take into account any effect which the observer had on the information studied. Newton and his followers believed that an objective reality not only existed, but could be known subjectively:

> If a tree falls in a forest, and there is nobody there to hear it, does it make a sound?

As science continued on its evolutionary course two theories had an enormous impact on it. The first of these was the work of Albert Einstein who, in his theory of relativity, described in detail the role of the observer in science. The work of Einstein was essential in modern physics because he began to describe the effect which the position of the observer had on the phenomenon studied. Einstein proved that there is no one objective reality which exists uninfluenced by the perceiver; further, that if there is an objective reality, it cannot be known without taking into consideration the act of perceiving it.

> The chief merit of the name "Relativity" is in reminding us that the scientist is unavoidably a participant in the system he is studying. Einsten gave "the observer" his proper status in modern science.[1]

An example that illustrates the importance of the observer's position is that of a boxcar traveling at 100 miles per hour. In the boxcar there are two people, one at the front of the car and the other at the back. If the person at the front of the car rolls a bowling ball at 10 miles per hour to the person at the back of the car, how fast is the bowling ball traveling? In order to answer this question, we must first know where the observer, who is doing the measuring, is located. If he is in the front of the boxcar, the bowling ball is traveling at 10 miles per hour away from him. If he is at the back of the boxcar, the bowling ball is traveling at 10 miles per hour towards him; however, if the observer is standing at the side of the railroad tracks, the bowling ball is traveling at 90 miles per hour. This example demonstrates the "relative" nature of scientific measurement.

In addition to the works of Einstein, Werner Heisenberg was able to build a theory which described the necessary influence of the scientist on the event(s) studied.

Heisenberg's Uncertainty Principle which states that it is impossible, at a given instant of time, to measure accurately both the position and the momentum of a fundamental particle — this is a basic law of nature which in crude language means whenever we try to measure something we change it.[2]

The acceptance of a relativity based model in the exact science of physics has generalized out into other fields including the social sciences.

We will see that unlike popular belief, people do not act upon the world, but instead, upon representations of the world. These representations are made or constructed based on what is perceived through the senses. We are never in direct contact with the world at large, but instead, we are always one step removed via the information being filtered through our senses. We therefore build maps of the world and act as though these maps are the world itself. Most people consider the map as actually being reality, instead of taking into account that these maps are only representations. Therefore, it is important to realize that the map is not the territory.

Important characteristics of maps should be noted. A map is not the territory it represents, but, if correct, it has a similar structure to the territory, which accounts for its usefulness.[3]

No two people create identical maps for the same territory. These maps are somewhat individualized and necessarily so. Most of us, however, having similarities in these maps, are able to agree upon the structure of the territory enough to have a consensus or shared reality. In considering these maps we need to make note of what Bandler and Grinder call constraints of the model or map. "The physical world remains constant, and our experience of it shifts dramatically as a function of our nervous system."[4]

There are three categories of constraint: neurological, sociological and individual.[5] Neurological constraints refer to those phenomenon that lie outside the range of our sensory experience, such as, sound is not perceivable by the human ear below 20 cycles per second or above 20,000 cycles per second. Also, the human eye can only detect wave forms between 380 and 680 milli-microns. In addition, neurophysiology tells us that the density of kinesthetic nerve receptors are higher on the outer extremities, such as the fingers or toes, than that of the receptors on the trunk of the body. Because of this, kinesthetic reception is neurologically constrained simply from one part of the body to the other. The most commonly noted confirmation of the nature of our neurological constraints is demonstrated by the very existence and extensive use of scientific measuring devices. Thermometers, electron microscopes, audio wave receptors, etc., all are devices which detect phenomenon that lie outside the range of our senses.

Sociological constraints are another way in which our maps of the world come to differ from the world at large. For instance, the Eskimo's existence depends largely upon the conditions of the weather, they therefore have 20 some odd words, to our few, to describe the physically constant phenomenon snow, thus, resulting in different maps for essentially the same territory.

The third way in which the map differs from the territory is determined by individual constraints. The uniqueness of individual personal histories and positions in the world based on the time/space coordinates will have an effect on the individual's map or model of the world. A person's own individual life experiences will have a bearing upon the maps he creates. Even two individuals with similar life experiences, such as being raised in the same family, country and/or culture, will have in actuality vastly different experiences due to their own position in space and time.

Anything that we as individuals perceive, believe, and/or have as items in our personal history, offer us both a vast storehouse of resources and a number of restrictions. This is the logical outcome of the fact that we build maps and, in doing so, consciously or unconsciously, by the very existence of the process of "modeling", select from an infinite variety of sensory experience, the items that will be represented in these maps.

Based upon the preceding information regarding the neurological, sociological, and individual constraints which have a direct effect upon the modeling processes and the models built by the individual person, we note that there are considerable, or even drastic differences between individual models or maps of the territory. We do not believe that there is any one model or that there is a right model. To borrow from the field of physics:

> Neils Bohr suggested that the search for one correct model was medieval, pre-scientific and obsolete. We can best understand sub-atomic events, he said, if we accept the necessity of allowing for more than one model.[6]

2

MODELING PROCESSES

There are three universal modeling processes: generalization, deletion, and distortion. These modeling processes have a direct effect upon the models built and allow us to grow, create, learn, and cope with day-to-day life; however, at times, these same processes can limit our experiences and thus limit our models of the world.

"Generalization is the process by which elements or pieces of a person's model become detached from their original experience and come to represent the entire category of which the experience is an example."[7] Effectively used, this process enables us to transfer learning from one context to another, such as in learning to drive an automobile. If not for generalization, each time you came to a new locale or bought a new car, you would have to again learn how to drive. Although at times there are minor adjustments, the process of generalization enables us to drive different cars and in new locations.

The process of generalization can serve as a limitation by stunting our creative ability. For example, a person who as a child, suffers a dog bite and from then on fears all dogs. In this case, the person generalizes from one specific situation in which he was bitten to an all encompassing fear of all dogs in any context. This situation is an example of the paradigm which accounts for most phobias.

A second mechanism which may allow us to cope effectively or to defeat ourselves is deletion. "Deletion is a process by which we selectively pay attention to certain dimensions of our experience and exclude others."[8] Deletion is the mechanism which enables one to avoid being overwhelmed by bombarding external stimuli. This process allows one to talk on the phone while standing in a noisy, crowded room. Deletion can also enable one to limit his growth, such as the spouse who believes he is being treated unfairly may delete his contribution to the unhealthy situation, thus eliminating any creative responses to enhance the relationship.

"The third modeling process is that of distortion. Distortion is the process which allows us to make shifts in our experience of sensory data."[9] Effectively used, this process allows us to create from fantasy, such as, the works of sculptures, novelists, and painters. Distortion is useful in planning a vacation, deciding what attractions to see, which clothes to pack, and which restaurants to visit. Distortion is also used in choosing a wardrobe by imagining which articles of clothing will go well together without having them present.

Distortion can be a means by which we limit our individual models of the world. Jealousy is often an example of distortion. The individual feeling the jealousy in many cases manipulates his perception of certain situations by using distortion. This manipulation of the facts allows the person to imagine his mate with someone other than himself and then begin to act as though the hallucination is real, instead of taking the initiative to check sensory experience to verify whether or not the feelings of jealousy are reality based.

We have determined thus far in this chapter that human beings create models or representations of the world. It is our belief that many of the limitations that clients bring to therapy with hopes of change are limits in the client's model of the world and not limits in the world itself.

3

PRESUPPOSITIONS OF THE MODEL

A great portion of this book will be devoted to presenting a model of therapy. This model has within it several presuppositions. One of the presuppositions is that choice is better than no choice. It is our goal when working with a client to increase his options or choices. To borrow from the field of systems theory, the law of requisite variety, which states the component within a system or system within a group of systems with the most variability controls the system. For our use, this means the person with the most options wins. Another presupposition is that when a person comes to therapy, he already has all the resources needed to make the desired changes. It is our belief that the task of the therapist is to assist the client in gaining access to these resources and making them available in the desired context. We also hold as a presupposition that a person always makes the best choice possible at each moment in time given the resources available.

We would like to state that by presupposition, we do not mean that these are true statements or truths of any kind, but only a useful way to proceed. As stated earlier, any belief or presupposition offers both a wealth of resources and a series of limitations. It is our belief that proceeding with the above-mentioned presuppositions gives the therapist and client options that other models do not.

4

REPRESENTATIONAL SYSTEMS

People do not act directly upon the world, but instead upon maps, models, or representations of the world. A way that these representations are coded is based upon the senses, that is, what one sees, hears, feels, smells, and tastes. The representational systems[10] are:

- (V) VISUAL
- (A) AUDITORY
- (K) KINESTHETIC
- (O) OLFACTORY
- (G) GUSTATORY

Although most people use all representational systems in day-to-day living, there is a tendency to specialize in one or two. For example, some people will have primarily the visual parameters of experience in consciousness, while others may have kinesthetic or auditory. Consciousness is defined here as everything that an individual is aware of at any moment in time.

One way of detecting which representational system a person has in consciousness is by listening to his language, the sentences that he generates, and noticing the predicates that he uses. The predicates in language are the verbs, adverbs, and adjectives and will in most cases presuppose one representational system. The representational system which is most commonly used is referred to as the "Primary Representational System."[11]

Below is a list of predicates and which representational system they belong to:

V	A	K	O	G
Perspective	Harmony	Vibrations	Fragrant	Bitter
Bright	Discuss	Fell	Smell	Stale
Clear	Listen	Soft	Pungent	Salty
Show	Tone	Euphoric	Stink	Taste
Dull	Hear	Firm	Reek	Fresh
Glimpse	Talk	Relaxed	Aroma	Sweet
Focus	Tune	Touch	Sour	Bland
Colorful	Shout	Tense		
Pretty	Loud	Pressure		
See	Call	Concrete		
Hazy	Sound	Grasp		
Look	Harp	Hurt		
Fuzzy	Scream	Irritate		
Picture	Quiet	Handle		
Shiny	Told	Clumsy		
Flash	Noisy	Smooth		
	Yell	Rough		
		Hard		
		Clammy		
		Awkward		

Kinesthetic:

Client: I really feel bad about my relationship with my husband. When he comes home my guts begin to churn, my stomach gets tied in knots and I feel really ill. You know, I can't get a grasp on just what's wrong, but I feel terrible.

Visual:

Client: I really don't see my marriage working out. When my husband comes home I look at him and can't picture us staying together very long. I just see my life as being brighter without him.

Auditory:

Client: There is real disharmony in my marriage. When my husband comes home and I hear his wimpering voice, I could just scream. You know when he trys to talk to me I just don't listen.

Olfactory:

Client: My marriage stinks. When my husband and I first met the relationship was good. It has since gone sour.

Gustatory:

Client: My relationship with my husband really leaves a bad taste in my mouth. What was once sweet has now gone stale.

In the aforementioned examples the content of the transcripts are basically the same, however, the actual description varies greatly depending on the client's primary representational system.

Meaning	Kinesthetic	Visual	Auditory
I (don't) understand you.	What you are saying <u>feels</u> (doesn't <u>feel</u>) right to me.	I <u>see</u> (don't <u>see</u>) what you are saying.	I <u>hear</u> (don't <u>hear</u>) you clearly.
I meant to communicate something to you.	I want you to be <u>in touch</u> with something.	I want to <u>show</u> you something (a picture of something).	I want you to <u>listen</u> carefully to what I <u>say</u> to you.
Describe more of your present experience to me.	Put me in <u>touch</u> with what you are <u>feeling</u> at this point in time.	<u>Show</u> me a <u>clear picture</u> of what you <u>see</u> at this point in time.	<u>Tell</u> me in more detail what you are <u>saying</u> at this point in time.
I like my experience of you and me at this point in time.	This <u>feels</u> really good to to me. I <u>feel</u> really good about what we are <u>doing</u>.	This <u>looks</u> really <u>bright</u> and <u>clear</u> to me.	This <u>sounds</u> really good to me.
Do you understand what I am saying?	Does what I am putting you <u>in touch</u> with <u>feel</u> right to you?	Do you <u>see</u> what I am <u>showing</u> you?	Does what I am <u>saying</u> to you <u>sound</u> right to you?

Bandler & Grinder
Structure of Magic
Vol. II, page 15

Algorithm for Identifying Primary Representational System

1. Listen to the sentences that the client generates.

2. Identify the verbs, adverbs, and adjectives (predicates) in the sentences.

3. Identify which representational system is presupposed by these predicates.

4. The system presupposed by the majority of the predicates is the primary representational system.

5

UNSPECIFIED VERBS

Unspecified verbs are a general class of predicates which do not presuppose any one representational system. When unspecified verbs are contained in a sentence, it is not possible to determine by the predicates which representational system the speaker is processing in. Since communication is redundant, the same information is available via several systems. We will further explore ways of gathering and utilizing this information in the section on "accessing cues."

Unspecified Verbs

Think	Sense
Know	Learn
Aware	Intuit
Experience	Change
Wonder	Remember
Notice	Believe
Understand	Consider

Client: I <u>know</u> that my marriage isn't going well, the experience just isn't the same. I often <u>wonder</u> how long it will last. I can <u>remember</u> when things were different, I just don't <u>understand</u>.

To use the same general content as used in the example(s) on primary representational systems, a dissatisfactory marriage, the above example is one of a client who, when describing her experience, uses unspecified verbs.

6

CONTEXTUAL CUES

The environmental context, in some cases, will have a direct effect on an individual's primacy of representational systems. A person might have primarily one representational system in consciousness in one situation, and another in a different situation.

Example:

Joe Stevens is a chemical engineer. When Joe is working on the job, his primary representational system is visual, which makes sense, given the nature of the job. Joe, however, when making love to his wife, has the kinesthetic portions of experience in consciousness, which also makes sense given the nature of love making. When discussing primacy of representational systems, the context is an important variable.

7

THE FIVE TUPLE

A calculus for ongoing experience is the Five Tuple. The Five Tuple is a representation of a person's experience at a specific moment in time. The Five Tuple stands for the five parameters of experience, that is: Visual, Auditory, Kinesthetic, Olfactory, and Gustatory.

Five Tuple = (V, A, K, O, G)

By using this method of analysis, one can gather a description of a person's subjective experience. All parameters of experience are not in consciousness at all times, consciousness is limited. George Miller, in his article, "The Magic Number 7 ± 2", states that a person can only have in conscious awareness 7 ± 2 chunks of information at one moment in time.[12] Therefore, only portions of the Five Tuple will be in the person's awareness.

Example:

> Susan Lee, standing in clover, looking across the field, smells the air and listens attentively to the birds singing.

One might represent this example as follows:

V – The sight of the field
A – The sounds of the birds singing
K – Out of consciousness
O – The odors and fragrances of the air
G – Out of consciousness

Portions of experience that are out of consciousness are represented in the brain, however, not at a conscious level at that moment in time. The parameters of the Five Tuple listed as "out of consciousness" could be brought into consciousness by using a technique known as overlap of representational systems.

A further distinction of the Five Tuple is internally versus externally generated experience. Externally generated experiences are things perceived as being seen, heard, felt, tasted, and smelt outside of ourselves. Internally generated experiences are those experiences that we create within ourselves, such as things imagined and remembered. A notation can be made on the Five Tuple with a superscript "i" for internal, and a superscript "e" for external.

Example:

V^i – Visual Internal
A^e – Auditory External
K^i – Kinesthetic Internal

8

OVERLAP OF REPRESENTATIONAL SYSTEMS

Overlap is the process of building a model of the world that includes all the parameters of the Five Tuple (V, A, K, O, G). In many cases, the resources a client needs in order to make the desired changes are stored in representational systems which are out of conscious awareness. In such cases, a client gaining access to the out of consciousness representational systems will not only give him more options, but also access to these resources. In overlap, one establishes bridges or synesthesias between representational systems. Overlap is accomplished by starting with the representational system in consciousness, finding a point of overlap or intersection, then guiding or leading the client to other systems.

Example:

As you feel (K) your feet walking (K) on the leaf covered ground, you can hear (A) the crunch (A) of the leaves and hearing the crunch (A), you might look (V) down and notice the color (V) of the leaves.

In this example, the client is led in guided fantasy from kinesthetic to auditory and auditory to visual. The use of guided fantasy will begin to build the synesthesias or bridges between representational systems. These bridges will generalize to other contexts, thereby giving him access to more resources.

Transcript

Client: I have this tight feeling in my stomach.

Therapist: Get in touch with that feeling and allow it to float up into a picture.

Client: Okay.

Therapist: What specifically is the picture of?

Client: It is a dark colored cloud.

Therapist: Okay. Now, take that picture of the cloud and change it into a pleasant, relaxed picture.

Client: Okay.

Therapist: What is the picture of?

Client: A piece of flowing white cloth, waving in the wind.

Therapist: Now, take that picture, reach out and pull it into your chest and as you do, make that picture into a feeling.

Client: Okay, I've got it.

Therapist: How do you feel in your stomach now?

Client: Relaxed.

Transcript

Client: When I get up in the morning and think about going to work, I begin to feel very ill.

Therapist: Is there a picture that goes along with that feeling of being ill?

Client: It's like there's a wall preventing me from going to work.

Therapist: Can you see the wall now?

Client: Yes.

Therapist: How are you feeling at this moment?

Client: Anxious, and a little nauseated.

Therapist: See the wall again, and notice the hole in the center.

Client: Yes, I can see the hole in the wall.

Therapist: Now walk through the hole in the wall.

Client: Okay.

Therapist: I'm wondering how you feel now.

Client: I'm feeling somewhat relaxed, and I'm no longer nauseated.

Therapist: When you awake tomorrow morning and begin to get ready for work you may feel somewhat ill. At that point, I want you to see the wall again, then notice the hole and walk through the hole. As you do you will feel relaxed, and, therefore, able to go to work.

Client: Okay.

In each of the aforementioned transcripts the therapist leads the client from an unpleasant kinesthetic state to a visual state. The therapist then has the client alter the visual experience so as to produce a more desirable kinesthetic outcome.

Algorithm for Overlap of Representational Systems

1. Identify the client's primary representational system.

2. Utilizing the client's primary representational system, build a description of the client's experience.

3. Locate an intersection point and begin to describe the client's experience in more than one representational system.

4. Switch your description to one which presupposes a different representational system.

5. Continue this process until all parameters of the 5 Tuple (V, A, K, O, G) are included in your description of the client's experience.

SENSORY EXPERIENCE

An essential in the art of face-to-face communication is being able to notice responses. By noticing responses we mean being able to see and hear the effects which your communication, verbal and/or non-verbal, has on the client. In many cases, the therapist misses much of the information offered to him by the client because his conscious awareness is at least partially distracted by internal processing, better known as "thinking". When the therapist is "thinking", his 7 ± 2 chunks of awareness are focused on internal experiences rather than external. Most people live day-to-day in a mixed state of consciousness with part of their awareness focused externally and part of their awareness focused internally.

Example:

$$V^e$$
$$E^i$$
$$K^i$$
$$O^e$$
$$G^i$$

One of the most effective strategies for doing psycho-therapy is to focus your 7 ± 2 chunks of consciousness exter-nally. Bandler and Grinder refer to this as "uptime."[13] Up-time allows the therapist to be in sensory experience and maximize his ability to systematically notice and utilize responses.

Example:

$$V^e$$
$$A^e$$
$$K^e$$
$$O^e$$
$$G^e$$

While in uptime, a person has no internal experience. In this state of consciousness a person does not make internal pictures or internal sounds, and is unaware of internal feel-ings. This allows the therapist to easily detect the informa-tion (communication) offered to him by the client. The up-time strategy is what don Juan refers to as "Stopping the World" in the writings of Carlos Castaneda.[14] We will later, in this volume, present an exercise which will allow the reader to enter uptime and utilize it.

ACCESSING CUES

The predicates only indicate which representational system a person has in conscious awareness; however, there are also behavioral cues that indicate in which representational system or series of representational systems a person is processing. These behavioral indicators are called accessing cues.[15] Accessing cues are a way that we, as human beings, focus neurologically on certain portions of subjective experience (V, A, K, O, G). For the most part, accessing cues work on an unconscious level and are not within conscious awareness. An individual, by carefully observing another person's accessing cues, can detect how he is processing information. Accessing cues and series of accessing cues are the very structure of subjective experience. There are two presuppositions underlying accessing cues.

1. Any occurrence in one part of a system (such as the neurological and biological system that makes up a human being) will necessarily affect all of the other parts of that system in some way. When the patterns

of interaction between the parts of the system are identified, the effects of the different parts of the system on one another can be predicted and utilized.[16]

2. In humans, all behavior (macro- and micro-) is a transformation of internal neurological processes, and, therefore, carries information about these processes. All behavior, then, is in some way communication about the neurological organization of the individual — a person can't not communicate.[17]

EYE MOVEMENT

Eye movements are an excellent behavioral indicator of a person's internal processes.[18] Although there are a great number of accessing cues, eye movement patterns are one of the most consistent and easy to detect. By watching a person's eye movements, one can easily detect in which representational system(s) he is processing information. It seems that the movement of the eyes stimulate the neuropathways to the brain, which makes available certain portions of experience. Unlike predicates, which allow one to determine which portions of experience are in consciousness, much of the processing which is done via accessing cues is out of a person's conscious awareness.

Eyes Up to Client's Left

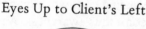

V^r

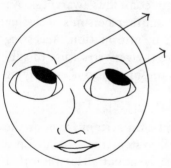

Visual Remembered
Visual Eidetic

Client has the experience
of seeing pictures from the
past.

Non-Dominant Hemisphere

Eyes Up to Client's Right

V^c

Visual Constructed

Client is constructing images, seeing things he has never actually seen.

Dominant Hemisphere

Eyes Straight Forward — Pupils Dilated

V
Visual

To determine which hemisphere is activated, watch which side of the body moves. If the left side of the body moves, the non-dominant hemisphere is being activated. If the right side of the body moves, it is the Dominant Hemisphere.

Eyes Horizontal Left

A^r

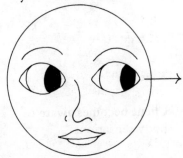

Auditory Remembered
Auditory Tape Loops

Client has auditory experiences from the past.

Non-Dominant Hemisphere

Eyes Horizontal Right

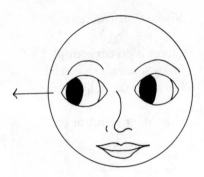

A^c

Auditory Constructed

Client is putting something to words and/or constructing things to say.

Dominant Hemipshere

Eyes Down Left

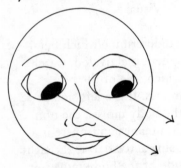

Ad

**Auditory Digital
Internal Dialogue**

Client is talking to himself.

Eyes Down Right

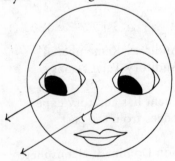

K

Kinesthetic

Client becomes aware of body sensations.

UP TO LEFT	(V^r) VISUAL REMEMBERED
UP TO RIGHT	(V^c) VISUAL CONSTRUCTED
STRAIGHT FORWARD DEFOCUSED (PUPILS DILATED)	(V) VISUAL (WATCH WHICH SIDE OF THE BODY MOVES FOR C OR R)
HORIZONTAL LEFT	(A^r) AUDITORY REMEMBERED
HORIZONTAL RIGHT	(A^c) AUDITORY CONSTRUCTED
DOWN TO LEFT	(Ad) AUDITORY DIGITAL
DOWN TO RIGHT	(K) KINESTHETIC

These generalizations hold true for most right-handed people, however, there may be some variations for left handers due to their differences in cerebral organization.

OLFACTORY AND GUSTATORY ACCESSING CUES

Flaring of the nostrils and taking a deep breath through the nose, as if smelling something, is an accessing cue for olfactory. Licking of the lips is an accessing cue for gustatory.

GESTURES

People will frequently point to the sense organ they are processing in, such as pointing to their eyes, ears, nose or mouth. When accessing kinesthetically, people generally touch themselves at the midline. In North American culture, a common accessing cue for internal auditory digital, or talking to oneself, is the telephone position. The telephone posture is head cocked to one side and holding one's hand to the side of the face as if holding a telephone receiver.

MINIMAL MUSCLE MOVEMENT

In many cases, people will minutely move the part of their body involved in the task they are accessing. For example, when a client is asked about the feel of his spouse's hair, the client might access that information by rubbing his fingers together, as if actually feeling the hair.

BREATHING CHANGES

Since all behavior is communication about the neurological organization of an individual, and human communication is redundant, the information available through eye movements are also available by other accessing cues. When a person is breathing high and shallow in the chest he is accessing visually. Breathing evenly in the diaphragm indicates auditory accessing. Kinesthetic accessing is accompanied by breathing deep and low in the stomach.

VOICE TONE/TEMPO

There are voice tone/tempo changes which accompany accessing in certain representational systems. When a person's voice raises in pitch, he is accessing visually; the person's rate of speech is also somewhat staccatic, as if talking between the pictures. Auditory accessing is accompanied by an even mid-ranged voice tone and a rhythmic tempo. Slow tempo, long pauses, and deep tone are characteristics of kinesthetic accessing.

11

LEAD SYSTEMS

In some cases, the client's primary representational system and accessing cues are mismatched. For example, the client may have kinesthetic as his primary representational system, indicated by listening to the predicates; however, he is accessing visually, indicated by accessing cues (e.g. eye movements). In this situation, the accessing cues are the "lead system"[19] and indicate that the client is deriving his feelings (K) from pictures (V). The client may only be aware of his primary representational system, whereas the lead system is out of consciousness. The relationship between the lead system and the primary representational system could be referred to as a synesthesia. This lead system and primary representational system or synesthesia is diagramed V/K.

Transcript

Client:	I	Eyes Shift Up and to the Left (V^r).
	feel so depressed.	Eyes Shift Down and to the Right (K^i).
Therapist:	What specifically do you feel depressed about?	
Client:	I don't know	Eyes Shift Up and to the Left (V^r).
	I just feel depressed.	Eyes Shift Down and to the Right (K^i).
Therapist:	What pictures do you see in your head?	
Client:		Eyes Shift Up and to the Left (V^r).
	I don't see anything.	
Therapist:	Allow your feelings of depression to intensify and then have those feelings float up into a picture.	
Client:		Eyes Shift Down and to the Right (K^i).
		Eyes Shift Up and to the Left (V^r).
	Okay.	
Therapist:	What do you see?	
Client:	My husband scolding me.	Eyes Shift Up and to the Left (V^r).
		Eyes Shift Down and to the Right (K^i).

In the aforementioned transcript, the client is deriving her feelings (K^i) from pictures (V^r) which are out of consciousness. The therapist, noticing the V/K synesthesia, elegantly uses overlap of representational systems to recover the picture (V^r) from which the unpleasant feelings (K^i) are derived. Once this is done, there are a number of ways to deal with the situation, which will be covered later in the book.

12

PACING AND LEADING

The first step in any therapeutic transaction is that of identifying and utilizing the client's model of the world. Pacing is meeting the client at his model of the world, which in turn establishes a deep sense of rapport.[20] Pacing is accomplished by feeding back to the client his verbal and/or nonverbal behavior, which creates a situation whereby the therapist functions as a sophisticated biofeedback machine.

In pacing, the therapist uses his own verbal and analogue behavior to match that of the client. The therapist tunes his output systems so as to synchronize with the output systems of the client. If an adequate pace has been established, the client will be experiencing, as sensory input via therapist's behavior, information which directly corresponds with his own output systems. The harmony established accounts for a certain sense of rapport and oneness.

Once an adequate pace has been established, the second step in the therapeutic process is that of leading the client to the desired goal(s). Since it is our belief that the state of inadequate resources are a direct result of either an impoverished or inappropriately contextualized model, the therapist's task is to lead a client to a model in which more resources are available.

Leading is a process by which the therapist begins to overlap behavior from the present state to the desired goal(s). The process of leading allows the therapist to assist the client in expanding his model, which allows for more behavioral and psychological flexibility and therefore more options and choices.

VERBAL PACING AND LEADING

There are a number of therapeutic patterns which allow the therapist to pace and lead the client verbally. Verbal pacing and leading is utilizing words in order to establish rapport and achieve desired goals.

Representational Systems

As we have previously discussed in the section on representational systems, a client will frequently describe his experiences based on sensory modalities: V, A, K, O, G. These descriptions of experience may vary greatly due to the client's primary representational system. In the case where the therapist and client share similar language, utilizing the same primary representational system, rapport is established. In some cases, however, the therapist and client having different primary representational systems find it difficult to communicate, almost as though they are speaking different languages. Failure in communication will often lead to confusion and mistrust. When the therapist uses the technique of pacing by using predicates which presuppose the same representational system as that of the client, rapport is achieved. This technique is known as matching predicates.

Once a pace is established, by matching predicates, the therapist can begin to lead the client by utilizing overlap of representational systems. This overlap of representational systems will expand the client's model of the world and allow fluidity in all the systems. In many cases, unfinished business or traumatic experiences are stored in representational systems which are out of the client's conscious awareness. In addition, resources needed in order to make desired changes may be stored in representational systems that are out of consciousness.

Transcripts

Kinesthetic:

Client: I have been <u>feeling</u> really depressed. I <u>feel</u> like I can't get a <u>handle</u> on anything.

Therapist: It seems to me that you want to get in <u>touch</u> with what is going on so that you can <u>get</u> the

feeling of once more having a <u>firm grasp</u> on your life.

Client: Yes, that's right.

Therapist: Well, let's begin by getting a <u>feel</u> for what you are <u>depressed</u> about.

Visual:

Client: I really <u>see</u> my life as going nowhere.

Therapist: <u>Focus</u> in on your goals so that we can <u>see</u> where you want to be.

Client: Hmm, let's <u>see</u>.

Therapist: Make a <u>clear picture</u> of where you want to be.

Auditory:

Client: I really need to <u>talk</u> about my problems.

Therapist: I <u>hear</u> what you are <u>saying</u>. What specifically do you want to <u>talk</u> about?

Client: Well, I've been troubled by my husband's drinking problem, but no one will <u>listen</u> to how it affects me.

Therapist: It <u>sounds</u> to me like we should <u>talk</u>. Why don't you start at the beginning and I will <u>listen</u>.

Client: That <u>sounds</u> great.

The following transcript is an example of pacing and leading via representational systems.

Transcript

Client: When I <u>look</u> at my life I <u>see</u> that I have accomplished nothing and when I <u>see</u> my friends doing better, well things just <u>look</u> bad.

Therapist: I <u>see</u> what you mean.

Client: I really want to go somewhere.

Therapist: Let's put things into <u>perspective</u>. Where do you want to go with your <u>life</u>?

Client: I would like to <u>picture</u> myself in a stable relationship with a satisfying job.

Therapist: Now, let's <u>focus</u> on relationships. Are you involved with anyone now?

Client: Yes. I have a girlfriend and she is really <u>pretty</u>.

Therapist: When you <u>picture</u> yourself with her, how do you <u>feel</u>?

Client: I <u>feel</u> good and close.

Therapist: Does that relationship <u>sound</u> like the kind of thing to pursue?

Client: Yes.

Therapist: Now, how about the job?

Client: Well, I'm in school now and when I finish I will be an attorney.

Therapist: When you <u>clearly</u> imagine yourself as an attorney do you <u>feel</u> good?

Client: Yes.

Therapist: What do you <u>tell</u> yourself about being a lawyer?

Client: Well, at times I <u>question</u> whether or not I can make it all the way through school, and when I <u>question</u> myself, I <u>tell</u> myself that I'll never make it.

Therapist: Do you think that you could give yourself a positive message such as, you'll make a fine attorney and can make it through school easily?

Client: I guess I could.

Therapist: Will you try it now, just to <u>see</u> how it <u>feels</u>?

Client: Okay.

[Pause]

Therapist: How did it turn out?

Client: Fine.

In the above transcript the therapist uses overlap of representational systems in order to lead the client through each system to isolate any objections that might stand in the way of the client achieveing his goal. As it was, the problem laid in the auditory system; more specifically, what message the client was telling himself.

Algorithm for Pacing and Leading
Via Representational Systems

1. Listen to the sentences that the client generates.

2. Identify the verbs, adverbs, and adjectives (predicates) in the sentences.

3. Identify which representational system is presupposed by the predicates.

4. Determine the primary representational system.

5. Decide what information you want to communicate to the client.

6. Code this information in sentences which contain predicates that presuppose the same representational system as the client's own primary representational system.

7. Deliver the sentences.

8. Locate an intersection point and begin to describe the client's experience in more than one representational system.

9. Switch your description to one which presupposes a different representational system.

10. Continue this process until all parameters of the 5 Tuple (V, A, K, O, G) are included in your description of the client's experience.

Unspecified Verbs

Another technique for verbally pacing a client is by using unspecified verbs. Unspecified verbs are predicates which do not presuppose any one representational system. Since these predicates are somewhat neutral in regard to representational systems, when used, they automatically will establish a pace.

Transcript

Client: I want to <u>feel</u> less <u>anxious</u> while driving my car.

Therapist: I <u>understand</u>.

Client: When I get behind the wheel and begin to drive, I just <u>feel overwhelmed</u>.

Therapist: So, my <u>understanding</u> is that when driving you would like to have that <u>experience</u> be different.

Mismatching Predicates

When predicates are mismatched a sense of rapport is not established and in many cases the outcome of this is that of confusion.

Transcript

Client: I <u>see</u> my life as going nowhere.

Therapist: How do you <u>feel</u> about that?

Client: I don't <u>feel</u> anything. I just want to get a <u>clearer perspective</u> on things.

Therapist: Well, an important aspect of therapy is to get in <u>touch</u> with your <u>feelings</u>.

Client: I really don't <u>see</u> what you mean.

Therapist: Why are you avoiding your <u>feelings</u>?

Client: I'm confused.

Descriptive Pacing

Descriptive pacing is a form of verbal pacing in which the therapist delivers a verbal description of the client's readily observable on-going behavior. When the client consciously or unconsciously hears a description of his behavior, which matches his actual behavior, a biofeedback loop is created. Once this biofeedback loop is created, as in all pacing, a sense of rapport develops.

The therapist can accomplish descriptive pacing in two ways. The first way is by observing and listening to the client and including in the on-going discussion statements which are readily verifiable in sensory experience. The second way of descriptive pacing is very similar but, in addition to describing observable behavior, the therapist uses a form of linguistic patterning which allows him to seem to have knowledge of the client's internal experiences. The linguistic patterning used is known as mind reading and generally involves the use of predicates which describe non-specifically the internal processes that each of us as human beings utilize.

For Example:

Remember	Think
Wonder	Experience
Know	Aware
Sense	Understand
Learn	Notice
Consider	Believe

As in all pacing, once an adequate pace is established, the therapist then can begin to lead the client toward the desired goal. Leading is particularly easy in descriptive pacing because the therapist need do little more than add a few suggestions into the descriptions. For most people, if you begin to make statements which are readily verifiable such as describing behavior or using mind reading to describe seemingly internal states, any additional suggestions which are attached to the description will be accepted along with those verifiable statements. People have a tendency to either accept or reject entire statements without taking the time to scrutinize each part of the statement. The verifiable portions of the statement will usually allow acceptance of the entire statement.

Example of Descriptive Pacing and Mind Reading

Client entered the office and after briefly looking around the room, sat in a chair next to the therapist. Client then sat quietly with his hands on his thighs, legs crossed, breathing deeply and rapidly.

Therapist: As you are sitting there with your legs crossed and your back resting on the chair, you're probably wondering what this therapy session will be all about.

Client: (Nods his head up and down as to signify agreement.)

Therapist: While you're sitting, listening to the sound of my voice, you can take a deep breath and begin to relax.

Client: (Takes a deep breath, exhales and uncrosses legs, taking a more relaxed body posture.)

Therapist: As you begin to relax comfortably you might want to begin to think about the issues which brought you in to therapy. And once you have considered what those issues are we can begin to discuss them.

Client: Ever since my son died I've been really depressed.

Therapist: Isn't it reassuring that you can sit there, remembering that certain experience and share those emotions, feeling more comfortable?

NON VERBAL PACING
Mirroring

Pacing can be accomplished non-verbally by directly adopting any portion of the client's analogue behavior thereby feeding that behavior back to the client. When the therapist directly adopts the client's behavior a mirror-like effect occurs, whereby the client witnesses his own behavior. This feedback loop creates a feeling of oneness, which generally leads to trust and rapport. There are a number of behavioral systems that can be effectively mirrored; these include: breathing rate and depth, voice tone and tempo, body posture and body movement. A therapist could easily establish rapport both at a conscious and more importantly unconscious level by matching the client's breathing. In this case, the client would see his therapist's chest rise and fall at the same rate and depth as his own.

As in all pacing, the therapist can easily shift to leading the client by overlapping present behavior to the desired behavioral state. If an adequate pace has been established the therapist can change his own behavior and the client will smoothly follow by adopting the new, desired behavior.

Case Study:

Client enters the therapist's office and takes a seat. Client sits with his arms crossed, both feet on the floor, and is breathing rapidly, taking shallow uneven breaths. The therapist introduces herself and too is seated. The therapist soon adopts client's body posture and breathing pattern. After the introductions are finished the client begins to discuss the problems which he is having in his life. The therapist continues to mirror client for a few minutes while listening to the problems. Once rapport is established the therapist begins to lead the client by deepening her own breaths and slowing down her own breathing rate. Therapist notices that the client follows the lead by adopting the same breathing pattern. Finally, the therapist uncrosses her arms and the client follows by doing the same.

In the above case study the technique of mirroring is utilized not only to establish rapport but also to assist the client in assuming a more comfortable and open analogue.

Algorithm for Mirroring

1. Choose a portion of the client's behavior.

2. Adopt that same behavior.

3. Maintain the adopted behavior for a period of three to seven minutes (rapport development).

4. Choose a desired behavioral outcome.

5. Adopt the new desired behavior.

6. Notice client's response.

Crossover Mirroring

In order to protect body integrity, the therapist needs to be careful not to match those behaviors that could be harmful to his health, such as direct matching of an asthmatic's breathing pattern or assuming an uncomfortable body posture as that of a person suffering from arthritis. Crossover mirroring is matching any one of the client's output channels with any output channel of a different system. Crossover mirroring is more covert than direct mirroring, and is less likely to be detected by the client. The therapist could, by using his voice tempo, match the breathing rate of the client: also, a therapist could tap his knee at the same rate the client rhythmically sways his foot.

Algorithm for Crossover Mirroring

1. Identify the piece of the client's ongoing behavior that you want to pace.

2. Choose which system in your own behavior that you want to pace the client with.

3. Synchronize your output system with that of the client's output system.

4. Notice the client's response.

By using mirroring and/or crossover mirroring, the therapist establishes rapport with the client both on a conscious and unconscious level. The therapist can also pace the client in more than one system by matching in several channels, such as matching predicates and mirroring body posture. There are an infinite number of combinations available for a creative therapist to directly and/or indirectly pace the client. Once an accurate pace has been established, the next step is to lead the client to a model of the world where he has more resources, choices, and options.

Pacing is integral to the overall therapeutic process. It is possible for the therapist to elegantly lead the client either verbally (via representational system(s)) and/or non-verbally (via analogical behavior). Since human behavior manifests itself as gestalts, leading a client by utilizing any of the aforementioned communication and information processing systems will necessarily have an effect on the entire individual.

13

META-MODEL

Borrowed from the field of transformational linguistics (Noam Chomsky) is the idea of deep structure and surface structure.

> Deep structure is the abstract structure, postulated as underlying a sentence, containing all information necessary for both the syntactic and semantic interpretations of the sentence. Surface structure is the grammatical relationship among words of an actually observed sentence.[21]

In short, the surface structure is what is spoken (written), while the deep structure is the actual meaning of the sentence.

We, as native speakers of the English language, have intuitions about the meaning of language. In many cases these intuitions supply us with meaning (deep structure) which is not formally displayed in the surface structure.

The car was built.

The surface structure of the prementioned sentence is what is actually written on the page. The deep structure, however, contains meaning which is not presented formally in the surface structure.

Deep Structure Representation: Past (Build [someone, car, with something])

Language is a representation of human experience and not the experience itself; language is a model. Since language is a model it is affected by the three universal modeling processes: deletion, distortion and generalization. In many cases, the language a client uses to describe his experience becomes detached from the actual experience. The meta-model is a series of formal linguistic operations which act upon the form rather than the content of language. The meta-model (Structure of Magic, Vol. I, Bandler and Grinder) works to reconnect the language to experience.

The meta-model distinctions fall into three natural groupings:

Gathering Information
Limits of the Speaker's Model
Semantic Well Formedness[22]

GATHERING INFORMATION

Gathering information is a category of meta-model questions which allows the therapist to elicit a fuller representation of the client's model of the world. The following subcategories, when utilized systematically, offer the therapist an opportunity to elicit a fuller, richer description of the client's experience.

Deletion

Deletion is meaning in the deep structure which is missing from the surface structure. The meta-model responses systematically recover the deleted material.

Simple Deletion

Client: I'm angry.
Therapist: At whom / about what?

Client: I'm hurt.
Therapist: About what?

Client: I feel sad.
Therapist: About what?

Client: I don't know.
Therapist: What specifically don't you know?

Client: I'm scared.
Therapist: Of what?

Lack of Referential Index

Lack of referential index is when a category of objects/ events is mentioned in the client's surface structure, however, the client does not refer to a specific object/event in sensory experience. Lack of referential index is an example of both deletion and generalization.

Client: People scare me.
Therapist: Which people specifically scare you?

Client: Cars are dangerous.
Therapist: Which cars specifically are dangerous?

Client: Women are evil.
Therapist: Which women specifically are evil?

Client: They're out to get me.
Therapist: Who specifically is out to get you?

Client: That's not right.
Therapist: What specifically is not right?

Client: Men are insensitive.
Therapist: Which men specifically are insensitive?

Comparative Deletion

Comparative deletion is when a client's sentence draws a comparison, however, the surface structure of the client's language does not indicate what the client is comparing.

Client: He's smarter.
Therapist: He's smarter than whom?

Client: She is more aggresive.
Therapist: She is more aggressive than whom?

Client: Debbie is the best.
Therapist: Debbie is the best compared to whom?

Client: Gabriel is least threatening.
Therapist: Gabriel is least threatening compared to
             whom/what?

Unspecified Verbs

Unspecified verbs are verbs in a sentence that do not indicate a full description of the action taking place. This term can also be used to describe verbs that do not specify which representational system the person is processing in.

Client: My husband hurts me.
Therapist: How specifically does your husband hurt you?

Client: My boss frustrates me.
Therapist: How specifically does your boss frustrate you?

Client: My children irritate me.
Therapist: How specifically do your children irritate you?

Client: My mother bores me.
Therapist: How specifically does your mother bore you?

Client: I know I'm tired.
Therapist: How specifically do you know you're tired?

Client: I realize my mistake.
Therapist: How specifically do you realize your mistake?

Nominalization

Nominalization is a process whereby a verb is changed into a noun, thus changing an ongoing process into a static object. In many cases, once the process of nominalization has occurred the client perceives the nominalized material as an unchangeable event/object instead of a changeable ongoing process. The process of nominalization is an example of distortion.

The Decision is Final.

In the above sentence the word decision is a nominalization; it is a verb (decide), which has been changed to function in the sentence as a noun. In this case, there is possibly no reason why the client can't redecide about the issue except that he perceives the decision as an unchangeable event. It is the first task of the therapist to assist the client in changing the nominalization back into a process. Once a verb has been nominalized much of the information concerning the process has been deleted. The second task of the therapist is to recover the deleted material. The material deleted from the aforementioned example might be:

> Who is Deciding?
> Deciding About What?
> Deciding When?
> Deciding Where?
> How Specifically Deciding?

To recover the deleted material the therapist can use the meta-model questions listed in the section on deletion.

The way to test for nominalization is to listen to/look at the surface structure of the sentence and identify the words functioning as nouns. If you cannot imagine being able to reach out and touch the nouns, they are nominalizations. For example, you can touch a chair, a table, a car, men and women, however, you cannot touch love, frustration, marriage, fear, and decision. Another test is to take the noun and place it after the phrase "an ongoing". If the phrase is logical, it is a nominalization.

An ongoing chair	)	
An ongoing table	)	<u>Nouns</u>
An ongoing car	)	
An ongoing love	)	
An ongoing decision	)	<u>Nominalization</u>
An ongoing fear	)	

Transcripts:

> Client: I want love.
> Therapist: You want loving from whom?

> Client: The decision is made.
> Therapist: What specifically are you deciding about?

> Client: There is frustration in my life.
> Therapist: What specifically is frustrating you?

> Client: My confusion is terrible.
> Therapist: What specifically is confusing you?

In the English language, many words ending in <u>ion</u> are nominalizations and they can easily be changed back to verbs by using their <u>ing</u> form.

LIMITS OF THE SPEAKER'S MODEL

Even though language is not experience, it is a powerful organizational tool which has a strong effect on the client's model of the world. In many cases, the client's language form creates limits which affect both the client's model of the world and behavior. The next section consists of a series of meta-model questions designed to challenge the limits of the speaker's model.

Universal Quantifiers

Universal quantifiers are those words which, as generalizations, stand for an entire category of which one example is a representative. Examples of universal quantifiers are: all, always, every, nobody and never. There are two ways to challenge universal quantifiers. One way is to use exaggeration in order to bring forth a response which puts the generalization into a more appropriate perspective.

Client: Nobody loves me.
Therapist: You mean nobody in the entire world?

Client: I'm always right.
Therapist: You mean always, every single time?

Client: All men stink.
Therapist: Every last one of them?

The second way to challenge universal quantifiers is to challenge the quantifier as a lack of referential index.

Client: Nobody loves me.
Therapist: Who specifically does not love you?

Client: I'm always right.
Therapist: When specifically are you right?

Client: All men stink.
Therapist: Which men specifically stink?

Modal Operators

In many cases, the client's language will indicate that, in certain situations, there is no choice. Since language is not experience, the lack of choice may not exist in the world at large but only in the client's model/language. By challenging modal operators, the therapist expands the client's model to include more choices. There are two challenges for modal operators; What would happen if you did (didn't)?, and, What stops you?

Modal Operators of Necessity

The modal operators of necessity are: must, it's necessary, have to, should, need to, and have got to.

Client: I have to clean the house before my husband gets home.
Therapist: What would happen if you didn't?

Client: I should finish this project by Friday.
Therapist: What would happen if you didn't?

Client: I need to quit drinking.
Therapist: What would happen if you did/didn't?

Modal Operators of Possibility

Can't and it's impossible are examples of modal operators of possibility.

Client: I can't quit drinking.
Therapist: What stops you from quitting? What would happen if you did?

Client: It's impossible to talk to my boss.
Therapist: What stops you? What would happen if you did?

Client: I can't concentrate on work.
Therapist: What stops you? What would happen if you did?

Each of the two challenges for modal operators will offer the therapist a different type of information. The challenge What stops you?, in most cases, allows the client to search into his personal history for an answer while What would happen if you did (didn't)? has the client project into the future.

SEMANTIC WELL FORMEDNESS

There are three general types of linguistic patterns which violate the semantic well formedness condition:

> Cause and Effect
> Mind Reading
> Lost Performative

These conditions are concerned with a type of distortion which impoverishes the client's model of the world and, therefore, his behavior.

Cause and Effect

Cause and effect is making the claim that there exist a cause and effect relationship between two not necessarily related events. In the field of therapy this becomes an important issue when a client claims that his emotions, feelings and/or behavior are caused by another person or thing. The appropriate meta-model response to challenge a cause and effect violation is How specifically?

Transcript

Client: My wife makes me angry.

Therapist: How specifically does your wife make you angry?

Client: My job makes me nervous.

Therapist: How specifically does your job make you nervous?

Client: My kids make me hit them.

Therapist: How specifically do your kids make you hit them?

Mind Reading

Mind Reading is claiming to have information about another person's internal state (thoughts, attitudes, likes and dislikes) without indicating how that information was obtained. The meta-model challenge for mind reading is the same as that for cause and effect How specifically?

Transcript

Client: I know he hates me.
Therapist: How specifically do you know he hates you?

Client: I know when my wife is upset with me.
Therapist: How specifically do you know when your wife is upset with you?

Client: I know I don't satisfy my spouse sexually.
Therapist: How specifically do you know that you do not satisfy your spouse sexually?

The information gathered by challenging both cause and effect and mind reading violations will frequently begin to provide insight into calibrated communication loops existing between people.

Lost Performative

In the English language, information about whom is speaking the sentence is almost always deleted from the surface structure. In front of or at the beginning of each utterance, one could put the statement "I am telling you that", which would indicate, in the surface structure, who is speaking the sentence. Many times a client will make a statement which is indicative of a personal belief system and present it as though it is a universal truth.

There are two ways to challenge violations of lost performatives; For whom?, and I hear that you are telling me that. The purpose of these challenges is to have the client own the beliefs as his own, and not universal truths.

Transcript:

Client: It's wrong to love two people at the same time.

Therapist: It's wrong for whom to love two people at the same time?

Client: Homosexuality is perverted.

Therapist: I hear that you are telling me that homosexuality is perverted.

Client: Alcohol reduces stress.

Therapist: Alcohol reduces stress for whom?

COMPLEX EQUIVALENCE

Complex equivalence is a special case of generalization in which the client equates a definition/meaning to a certain behavior or set of behaviors which is not necessarily true. Complex equivalence is similar to mind reading in that the client claims to have knowledge of another persons's internal state(s). In complex equivalence, however, the client claims to have acquired this knowledge via sensory based distinctions and the behavior may or may not be an indicator of that internal state. There are two steps to challenging a complex equivalence:

1. Challenge the generalization by asking the client if the generalization is always true.

2. If the client agrees that the generalization is always true, the next step is to switch referential index. In switching referential index, you hold the generalization constant; however, you change the role of the people involved. In most cases, this new generalization will not hold true and as such gives the therapist new information to explore.

Transcript

Client: When my daughter raises her voice . . . she is angry at me.

Therapist: Does you daughter raising her voice always mean that she is angry at you?

Client: No.

Therapist: When specifically does it mean that she is angry at you?

Transcript

Client: Jenifer frowns at me . . . she is disappointed in me.

Therapist: Does Jenifer frowning at you always mean that she is disappointed in you?

Client: Yes.

Therapist: Does your frowning at Jenifer always mean that you are disappointed in her?

Client: No, that's a different situation.

Therapist: How specifically is that a different situation?

META-MODEL AND UNCONSCIOUS COMMUNICATION

In our presentation of the meta-model, we stressed using the model in order to reattach language to experience, particularly by eliciting from the client a fuller linguistic representation. One advantage of systematically using the meta-model is being able to breakdown complex linguistic representations into smaller chunks. Although the meta-model when used to unpack language is most efficient, it would be unfortunate for the therapist to learn this model and utilize it only on the verbal component of human communication. As indicated in the section on accessing cues and pacing, the verbal portions of communication are but one system which we as human beings use to communicate. If the therapist uses sensory experience to notice nonverbal responses he will soon notice that to each question asked, the client will respond not only verbally, but also nonverbally.

When the therapist utilizes questions in order to establish well formed goals and/or uses the meta-model to unpack communication, the client will be responding verbally via language and non-verbally via accessing cues. The accessing cues offer a vast amount of information on how the client consciously and/or unconsciously structures subjective experiences. The therapist, by noticing these patterns, will not only be able to detect which recources and problems a client has, but also the structure of how they occur. It is possible for a therapist, by utilizing sensory experience, to detect via predicates and accessing cues series of sensory representations. These series of representations are the building blocks of subjective experience and are known as "strategies."[23]

Transcript

Client: I'm so angry.

Therapist: What specifically are you angry about?

Client:	Well, when I think	Eyes Shift Up and to the Left (V^r).
	about my mother	Eyes Shift Horizontal and to the Left (A^r).
	I get angry.	Eyes Shift Down and to the Right (K^i).
Therapist:	How specifically do you get angry?	
Client:	I'm not sure	Eyes Shift Up and to the Left (V^r).
	I just get	Eyes Shift Horizontal and to the Left (A^r).
	angry.	Eyes Shift Down and to the Right (K^i).

In the above transcript the therapist uses two questions from the meta-model, and, while noticing the accessing cues and predicates, is able to elicit the exact structure of how the client gets angry. The client makes a remembered visual image, hears an auditory tape loop, then becomes overwhelmed by anger. The visual and auditory portions of this sequence are out of consciousness for the client, however, he knows that the anger is somehow associated with his mother. Upon further exploration, it is revealed that the client remembers a picture of his mother scolding him, hears her voice yelling at him, and then feels angry. The sequence is diagramed:

$$V^r - A^r - K^i$$

14

UNCONSCIOUS FILTERING

There are times when the therapist asks the client a question and the client responds that he doesn't know the answer. In some cases, the client actually may not have the information available consciously; however, the information is stored in the unconscious mind. It has been proven that information, thought to be either not available or forgotten by a person, can be retrieved by such techniques as free association and hypnosis. Other techniques for acquiring information, bringing it into consciousness, are those of asking the client to guess, tell you a lie or by saying: If you did know the answer what would it be? These techniques free up the filtering device of the conscious mind as well as take away the burden of needing to be "correct" with the answer.

Transcripts

1) Client: I'm scared.
   Therapist: Of what?
   Client: I don't know.

Therapist: Well, then guess.
Client: Of losing my husband's love.

2) Therapist: What specific change would you like for
            yourself today?
   Client: I don't know.
   Therapist: Well, if you did know, what would it be?
   Client: I guess I would like to be more assertive with
             women.

3) Therapist: How did you feel when your boss chewed you
            out last week?
   Client: I don't know.
   Therapist: Come on, how did you feel?
   Therapist: Well, if you're not sure, then tell me a lie
            about how you felt.
   Client: I felt real hurt.

4) Therapist: What color was the house that you were
            raised in?
   Client: I can't remember.
   Therapist: Guess.
   Client: White.

15

GOALS IN PSYCHOTHERAPY

There are numerous ways of setting goals in the psycho-therapeutic context. There are, however, certain essential questions which not only allow the therapist to work with the client on setting specific treatment goals, but also assist in gathering the information necessary to implement the desired change. The following are questions which, when used as a general framework, help in gathering information and setting specific achievable goals:

1. What specific change do you want for yourself?

This question sets the initial goal(s) or outcome(s) for the therapeutic sessions. Within this question lies the presupposition that the client wants to make a change and that change is for himself. In order for a specific change to follow the well formedness conditions discussed in the meta-model, the desired change must be in the client's perceptual viewpoint of a specific issue or to be more global in his subjective experience. The therapist who is willing to accept, as a therapeutic goal, a client's desire to either change another individual's behavior or to alter a specific situation which is out of the client's control has set the sessions up for failure. It is extremely important that the therapeutic setting is designed in such a way that the therapist communicates to the client, in the initial goal setting stage of treatment, that the purpose of therapy is that of change on the part of the client. This not only expedites the therapeutic process, but tends to diminish the chances of therapy becoming merely a rent-a-friend.

2. What will having this change do for you?

Many times a client will desire to make a change which would be useless to have. This question requires that the client consider what he could do/have with the change that he could not do/have without it. In addition, this question can be used to change a previously ill formed outcome into a well formed outcome.

Transcript

Client: I want my husband to be kinder.
Therapist: What specifically would having your husband be kinder do for you?
Client: I would feel more relaxed.

In the above transcript an ill-formed outcome, wanting a kinder husband, is successfully converted to a goal which is achievable, relaxation.

3. In which context do you want that change?

A client may desire a change with little or no consideration made to the exact context(s) in which the change is desired. It is important for the therapist to assist the client in making the changes necessary, but, of utmost importance is having that change occur only in the appropriate situations.

Many times changes are made which generalize randomly across numerous contexts in a hit or miss fashion. When change is implemented in this generalized manner the change may be very appropriate in some of the contexts and totally inappropriate in others. The therapist, when precisely and clearly delineating the appropriate context(s), can implement change without negatively affecting the total-person ecology of the client.

4. How will you know when you have made that change?

The client often desires to remain in therapy for longer than necessary because he is unaware that his goals have been attained. Internal and external indicators of change are essential in the goal setting process and can serve two purposes: the first purpose is to allow the client to know when the goal has been achieved and the second purpose is that of acting as a convincer. The therapist can, by using the above question, elicit from the client, either by verbal description or direct behavior, the internal or external responses and/or behavior which allows the client to know that the goals are achieved. The indicator may be a certain body sensation, body posture, or possibly the client's internal dialogue. For some clients, resources (such as confidence) may be nothing more than a particular feeling or breathing pattern. In addition to indicators of goal achievement, there are situations which are very similar in function, however, what is needed is a particular internal or sometimes external state which convinces the client that a change or resource is available. For many clients having a command of certain knowledge is indicated by a particular feeling, a way of seeing things, or an internal voice.

5. What resources do you need in order to achieve that goal?

Present State + Resources = Desired State/Goals.

The above question when asked assists the client in searching through personal history for experiences in which the resource needed to make the desired change existed. This is accomplished by having the client float back in time and to some degree reexperience a particular memory. In other cases, the client may be asked to utilize a resource which was learned by watching or hearing another individual perform a specific task or handle a situation in a successful way. A third method to gain access to resources is by the use of imagination. The therapist may assist a client in gaining access to the resource needed by having the client imagine having that resource and then allowing himself to become immersed in that imaginary experience so as to learn and remember the resource.

Transcript on Goals in Psychotherapy

Therapist: What specific change do you want today?

Client: I don't know, I wish I was a bear.

Therapist: What would being like a bear do for you?

Client: Then I would be strong and assertive.

Therapist: In what context do you want to be strong and assertive?

Client: I would like to be assertive enough to ask my boss for a raise.

Therapist: How do you know when you're being assertive?

Client: I feel kind of tingly, like energy in my chest.

Therapist: Can you remember a time in your life when you were assertive?

Client: Sure, I felt very assertive when I was editor of the college paper.

Therapist: Continue to float back in time and allow yourself to intensely feel the assertiveness.

Client: Okay.

Therapist: Can you feel the tingling of energy in your chest?

Client: Yes.

Therapist: Now, memorize that feeling and allow yourself to take that feeling with you. In your mind imagine yourself asking the boss for a raise, remembering that you have that feeling in your chest.

              . . . Pause . . .

Client: Okay, I have it.

Therapist: Were you able to remain assertive while asking for the raise?

Client: Yes.

16

EXEMPLARY CHAPTER TRANSCRIPT

Jerry is a 37 year old, white collar worker who was referred by his employer. The client had a presenting problem of deteriorating work performance and work attendance.

Client:	Enters office and takes a seat opposite the therapist	The client is seated in the chair in an upright position with both feet on the floor. The client has a sweating forehead and is rubbing his hands together. The client's breathing is rapid and shallow.
Therapist:	(Therapist introduces herself). What changes would you like to make for yourself?	The therapist paces the client by assuming the same body posture and breathing pattern. (Within the question posed by the therapist lies the pre-

		supposition that the client wants a change and the change is for him.)
Client:	Instead of feeling so anxious, I would like to feel more comfortable.	(The client identifies what change he wants for himself. Question #1 from the section on "Goals".)
Therapist:	How specifically do you feel anxious?	(The therapist paces the client by matching predicates. The therapist has the client more completely specify the verb <u>feel</u> by asking the meta-model question — "how specifically?")
Client:	I	Eyes shift up and to the right (V^c)
	just really feel anxious.	Eyes shift down and to the right (K^1).
Therapist:		(The therapist observes that the client's lead system is visual and primary representational system is kinesthetic.)
Therapist:	When specifically do you feel anxious?	(The therapist begins to systematically challenge the deletion occuring in the surface structure of the client's language.

		The therapist continues to pace the client by matching predicates.)
Client:		The client crosses both his legs and his arms.
Client:	All the time.	
Therapist:		(The therapist continues to pace the client by assuming the changed body position, crossing her legs and her arms. The therapist continues to match the client's breathing.)
Therapist:	All . . . the time every single minute?	(By exaggeration, the therapist challenges the universal quantifier <u>all</u>.)
Client:	Well, no not really.	(The client responds to therapist's challenge of universal qualifier.)
Therapist:	Then when specifically?	(The therapist uses the meta-model question, "when specifically?" to challenge the deletion in the client's language.)
Client:	When I think about my financial situation.	Eyes shift up and to the right (V^c). Eyes shift down and to the right (K^i).

| Therapist: | | (The therapist notices that the client specifies the unspecified verb <u>think</u>, analogically by the accessing cue V^c.) |

| Therapist: | What specifically is troublesome about your financial situation? | (The therapist continues to gather information by using the meta-model question, "what specifically?", to challenge deletion.) |

Client:	The economy appears so bleak and,	Eyes shift up and to the left (V^r).
	when I see my wife and children spending money so foolishly,	Eyes shift up and to the left (V^r).
	I feel very anxious.	Eyes shift down and to the right (K^i).

| Therapist: | | (Therapist notices that the client uses the same lead system (V) and the same representational system (K) as when originally describing his anxiety. The same V-K pattern permeates throughout the problematic context.) |

| Therapist: | Are you having a hard time making your financial obligations? | (Therapist continues to pace the client by matching predicates, <u>Hard</u> K. Also, the therapist con- |

		(Therapist continues to gather information by recovering deleted material.)
Client:	No, not yet.	
Therapist:	Well then, how specifically do you get anxious?	(Therapist continues to use the meta-model to gather information.)
Client:	When I sit down and look at the bills	Eyes shift up and to the left (V^r)
	or see my family spending money	Eyes shift up and to the left (V^r)
	I just	Eyes shift up and to the right (V^c)*
	feel anxious.	Eyes shift down and to the right (K^1)
	In fact, I sometimes miss work because	Eyes shift up and to the left (V^r)
	I'm so anxious	Eyes shift down and to the right (K^1).
Therapist:		(*Therapist notices a visual constructed image V^c out of client's awareness*) (Therapist also notices that the client again uses a visual lead system and a kinesthetic representational system. The client has a strategy

which allows him to become overwhelmingly anxious in the context of bills and financial matters. This anxiety leads to absenteeism which in turn jeopardizes his financial situation, a self fulfilling prophesy.)

Therapist: When you look at the bills what specific picture do you see in your head just before you begin to feel anxious?

(Therapist asks the client to bring unconscious visual constructed image into consciousness by slowing down the series of internal representations.)

Client: Hmm, I never thought about it before.

Let's see.   Eyes shift up and to the right (V^c)

I imagine that I see myself   Eyes shift up and to the right (V^c)

losing my job and not being able to pay the bills.   Eyes shift down and to the right (K^1).

Therapist: Are there any other pictures?   (Gathers information.)

Client: At times I see myself   Eyes shift up and to the right (V^c)

losing everything, be-   Eyes shift down and to

	cause there is no money.	the right (K^i).
Therapist:	Are you presently and have you in the past met your financial obligations?	(Gathers information.)
Client:	Yes.	
Therapist:	Has there been any spending pattern changes with yourself or your family?	(Gathers information.) Therapist begins to lead the client by slowing her breathing rate and uncrossing her legs and arms. The therapist notices that the client follows by doing the same.
Client:	No.	
Therapist:	So, my understanding is that when you see yourself paying bills or considering your financial situation you want to feel more relaxed.	(Therapist paces the client by matching lead and representational systems and secures precise goals, Question Nos. 1 and 3 from the section on "Goals".)
Client:	That's right.	(Acknowledges goal.)
Therapist:	What would feeling comfortable in that situation do for you?	(Therapist continues to secure goal, Question No. 2 from the section on "Goals".)

Client: I would feel more re-
             laxed with my family
             and with my job.

Therapist: How would you know   (Therapist continues to
             when you've made   secure goals with Ques-
             that change?   tion No. 4 from the sec-
                                    tion on "Goals".)

Client: My stomach would   Eyes shift down and to
             be calm and my fore- the right (K^i).
             head dry.

Therapist: What specifically   (Therapist asks the client
             would you need to   what resources he would
             feel relaxed while   need to achieve goal,
             paying your bill?   Question No. 5 from
                                   "Goals" section.)

Client: I don't know.

Therapist: Has there ever been   (Therapist asks the client
             a time when you felt to search his own person-
             relaxed while paying al history for the appro-
             your bills?   priate resource.)

Client: Yes, about a year ago. Eyes shift down and to
                                    the right (K^i).

                                    Eyes shift up and to the
                                    left (V^r).

                                    (Client uses kinesthetic
                                    K^i as a guide to find a
                                    scene V^r when he felt
                                    relaxed.)

Therapist:	How were things different then than they are now?	
Client:		Eyes shift up and to the right (V^r) and then flick, shifting up and to the left (V^c). (Client visually compares current situation with scenes from past.)
Client:	We were saving money on a regular basis.	(Client finds the resource relaxation as a result of saving money.)
Therapist:	Can you see yourself saving money now and would saving money help you to feel more comfortable.	(Therapist assists the client in taking the resource from his personal history and using the resource in the present situation.)
Client:	Yes.	Eyes shift up and to the right (V^c). Eyes shift down and to the right (K^1).
Therapist:	How much would you need to save in order to feel comfortable.	(Therapist gets the client to be specific about the parameters of the resource state.)
Client:	$50.00 a week.	Eyes shift up and to the right (V^c).

		Eyes shift down and to the right (K^i).
Therapist:	Is that a reasonable goal?	(Therapist checks to see if this new arrangement violates the client's personal ecology.)
Client:	Yes.	
Therapist:	So, what's going on with your job?	(Therapist gathers information.)
Client:	Well, nothing much.	Eyes shift up and to the left (V^r).
	I really like my job.	Eyes shift down and to the right (K^i).
	However, at times I just can't go to work.	(Client uses modal operator of possibility.)
Therapist:	What stops you from attending work?	(Therapist challenges modal operator of possibility "can't", by using meta-model question "What stops you?".)
Client:	I guess I was caught up in a vicious circle.	Eyes shift up and to the left (V^r).
	I'd get anxious when	Eyes shift down and to the right (K^i).
	thinking about the bills	Eyes shift up and to the right (V^c).

	then feel too sick to work.	Eyes shift down and to the right (K^1).
Therapist:	Will saving money help you to feel more comfortable with you, with your job, and also with your family?	(Therapist checks to find out if the addition of the resource into the context of bills and finances will then make the desired change in the context of job and family.)
Client:	Yes.	
Therapist:	Now, go through the situation of paying bills next month, in your head, knowing that you have this new arrangement.	
Client:		Eyes shift up and to the right (V^c). Eyes shift down and to the right (K^1).
Therapist:		(Therapist notices that client's breathing rate remains even, muscle tone remains relaxed, and skin color is unchanged.)
Therapist:	How did you feel?	
Client:	Fine, relaxed and calm.	Eyes shift down and to the right (K^1).

Therapist: Is there anything else   (Ecological check.)
             that you want to talk
             about today?

Client: No.

PART II

You can pretend anything and master it.

Milton H. Erickson, M.D.

17

ANCHORING

ANCHORING

In the most general sense, an anchor is any stimulus which elicits a consistent response. The major difference between the concept of anchoring and "stimulus-response" theories of behavior is that the establishment of an anchor does not require reinforcement.[24]

Experience is stored in gestalts and the reintroduction of any portion of the gestalt, or whole experience, whether it be internal or external, will re-elicit the entire gestalt. The idea of anchoring is consistent with Karl Pribram's theory of holographic memory; that is, memory works very much like a hologram. A hologram is a three dimensional image which is created by recording the interference pattern of light waves reflected from an object or scene. In a hologram, any portion of the film will reproduce the entire image. In Pribram's holographic model of the brain, the cerebral cortex works like a hologram. In this model, information is stored in the form of neuronal patterns much in the same way that images are stored in the form of wave patterns in a visual hologram. This is a different approach to the study of neurology, because it puts emphasis on the process of brain function instead of localization. The hologram easily explains the research findings that indicate that information in the brain is infinitely cross referenced.

Memory is stored in gestalts and the piece of the whole, reintroduced, which elicits the response is called an anchor. Any portion of the 5 tuple, Ad (V, A, K, O, G), can serve as an anchor, thereby eliciting the entire 5 tuple. It is important to keep in mind that consciousness is limited and although the anchor elicits the entire 5 tuple, it is possible that only a portion of the 5 tuple will be within the client's conscious awareness.

There are certain cultural anchors to which most members of the culture involved will respond. Some examples of cultural anchors occuring in the United States are: the American flag, the national anthem, the red, yellow and green lights on a traffic signal, and the red stop sign. There are anchors which are consistent in the area of religion, such as: the Roman collar (worn by many priests and ministers), the crucifix, the Star of David, and the sign of the cross.

There are numerous anchors which elicit responses (5 tuple) from an individual's own personal history. For some people the smell of baking bread or walking into the house where they grew up may elicit a powerful response from their childhood. Songs are anchors and in many cases will re-elicit sensory representations of the times when they were popular. In a similar fashion, souvenirs from past vacations and mementos collected from meaningful relationships are anchors which may elicit as responses representations of those past experiences.

Words are powerful anchors and the way that human beings make sense out of the meaning of words is by searching their own personal histories for the 5 tuple to which the word is connected (anchored). The process of connecting words to their meaning is called transderivational search.

$$Ad \ (V, A, K, O, G)$$

Ad = Apple

V = Color of the Apple
A = Crunch of the Apple when bitten
K = Feeling of the Apple
O = Aroma of the Apple
G = Taste of the Apple

Since words are anchors, people are to some degree experiencing what they are communicating. This phenomen holds true whether the person is speaking or listening.

In the field of psychotherapy, anchoring is a profoundly useful tool in assisting clients to change. Anchoring allows the therapist to systematically stabilize states of consciousness. Since it is our belief that a client already has the resources necessary to make changes, the therapist by anchoring can make those resources available in the desired context. The therapist can stabilize (anchor) the appropriate 5 tuple by inserting a specific stimulus, such as touch, sound, or gesture into the 5 tuple and by reinserting that specific stimulus (touch, sound, or gesture) reaccess the desired 5 tuple and the resources which lie within the parameters of that 5 tuple. It is important in reaccessing a 5 tuple to duplicate the original anchor as closely as possible. If the anchor varies from the original anchor the therapist will then elicit only a portion of the original response. It seems that anchors follow the same variation gradients as the classical conditioning paradigms.

Precision in anchoring is based on the therapist's ability to notice and utilize the client's responses. There are certain non-verbal indicators which vary enough from state of consciousness-to-state of consciousness to allow the therapist to detect the response he is eliciting and/or re-eliciting. Some of these indicators are: facial muscle tone, voice tone, lip size, skin color, and breathing depth and rate. It is essential for the therapist to anchor the client just as the experience is expressed to its fullest.

Transcript:

Therapist: What specific change would you like?

Client: I would like to feel more confident.

Therapist: Can you recall a time in which you felt very confident?

Client: Yes.

Therapist: I would like you to get in touch with that feeling now and nod your head when you feel confident.

Therapist: (Observes the client's lips swelling slightly, breathing rate increases, skin color deepens.)

Client: [Nods.]

Therapist: (Reaches over and gently touches the client on the right wrist.)

Therapist: Come back to the here and now (the statement was delivered so as to clear the client's consciousness.)

Client: (Pause)

Therapist: (Once the client has returned to the here and now, and has sufficiently regained his "normal" state of consciousness, the therapist

once again touches the client on the right
wrist and notices that the client has re-experienced the same response, i.e., confidence.)

In the above portion of this transcript the therapist has
the client search his personal history for the resource (confidence). Once the therapist has assisted the client in gaining
access to that resource, the therapist stabilizes (anchors) the
resource with a touch on the right wrist. The therapist then
has the client clear consciousness and tests the anchor by
again touching the client on the right wrist. Since a strong
anchor has been established, the therapist notices the client
re-experiencing the same state of consciousness (confidence).
The therapist verifies that the state of consciousness is being
re-experienced by noticing certain minimal cues, such as:
swelling of lips, deepening of skin color and increased breathing rate.

Transcript:

Therapist: In what context would you like to have the
resource confidence?

Client: I would like to feel confident in raising my
children.

Therapist: Take a moment now and think of a situation
in the future that would require parenting
skills.

Client: Okay.

Therapist: Does having confidence improve that specific
situation?

Client: Yes.

Therapist: Continue to imagine that experience in the future knowing that you now have available to you the resource confidence. (As therapist is talking, he reaccesses the resource confidence by again touching the client on the right wrist.)

(Pause)

Therapist: What is the first thing you would see, hear or feel that would let you know that you are in a situation that requires confidence?

Client: I would hear one of my children crying.

Therapist: Imagine the sound of your children crying.

Client: Okay. I can hear them.

Therapist: (As the client is hearing the sound of his children crying, the therapist fires the anchor for confidence by touching him on the right wrist.

Client: Now imagine a time in the future that would require parenting skills and go through that situation with your resource confidence.

Therapist: (Verifies that the client is re-experiencing resource confidence in the situation parenting skills by observing minimal cues, i.e. swelling of lips, increased breathing rate, deepening of skin color.)

Therapist: Did you get the outcome that you wanted in that situation?

Client: Yes.

Therapist: Is there any other resources that you need in
the situation of parenting skills?

Client: No.

Once the therapist has anchored the appropriate resource,
he can assist the client in making that resource available in
the desired context by stimulus-stimulus conditioning. That
is, tying the anchor which formerly elicited the desired resource, to the context in which the resource is needed. The
context then becomes the anchor for the resource, thereby
making the resource available in that context. This process is
referred to as "future pacing."[25]
In the aforementioned transcript, the therapist establishes
an anchor for the resource confidence by touching the client's
wrist while he is experiencing the resource. During the future
pacing step the therapist asks the client for a naturally occurring indicator which lets him know that he is in the context
of parenting skills. The client chose the sound of his children
crying as the indicator and the therapist then fires the resource
anchor while the client is imagining the crying. By stimulus-
stimulus conditioning the crying then elicits the confidence,
thereby putting the resource in the desired context. Future
pacing automates the anchoring process by having the context
automatically elicit the desired resource.
In some therapies, the therapist works in order for the
client to make changes, however, the changes made are only
available in the therapist's office, treatment center or hospital.
These changes may be useful for the client in coping with his
therapist, but where the changes are needed are in the real
world of day-to-day life. Future pacing, tying the resource to
something in the client's day-to-day life, ensures that the
changes not only generalize to real life situations, but, more
specifically, to the situations where they are needed.

It is our belief that states of consciousness are, for the most part, neither positive nor negative. However, their usefulness and appropriateness are judged only in respect to the context(s) in which they occur, and/or the outcome desired. We also believe that behaviors and experiences are not maladaptive in themselves, but only in respect to their contexts.

18

PARTS

Many schools of psychotherapy use the concept of "parts." Such schools divide the whole individual into a specific number of parts, and each part is either assigned a specific function or given a behavioral description. In some cases, the parts can never be directly encountered, such as the ID and Superego in psychoanalysis. In other cases, the parts have specific behavioral descriptions and are considered to be directly observable: Parent, Adult and Child in Transactional Analysis.

Below is a list of parts and their appropriate schools of psychotherapy.

Satir	TA	Psycho-analysis	Gestalt	Hypnosis
Blamer	Parent	ID	Topdog	Conscious
Placater	Adult	Ego	Under-	Unconscious
Super	Child	Super	dog	
Reason-		Ego		
able				
Distracter				

Using a parts model is an efficient and effective way to proceed in psychotherapy, however, some therapists believe that these artificially assigned distinctions actually exist in the world as opposed to being a way of talking about experience and organizing it; the map is not the territory. One way of creating maps is by labeling or naming, which a parts model does. The process of labeling parts and then proceeding in treatment utilizing this parts model is similar to nominalizing, that is, changing the ongoing process of psychological and neurobiological functioning into a static event. Many therapists find that organizing the client's behavior into parts tends to restrict flexibility by forcing the client to behave in the position of one part or another and not having the fluidity to combine the behaviors. An example of this from the school of T.A. is that of not being able to act like a parent and a child at the same time. Another way to formulate the idea of parts is to consider the word which is used to label the part as an anchor, for example: the word "Parent", for some people, is an anchor for a certain experience and/or behavior.

It is possible that the labeling which occurs in a parts model becomes so rigid that the parts tend to take on a life of their own, even to the point of excluding other parts. In such extreme cases, the client may organize himself so completely in the parts model that each part becomes a personality of its own. This may at times explain the phenomenon known as multiple personality.

One could consider parts as being specific 5 tuples. By using the 5 tuple model it is possible to get a precise description of a client's subjective experience at any moment in time. This description can allow a therapist to begin to organize in a similar way to that of a parts model, however, since the 5 tuple gives a more behaviorally oriented description there is less room for the slippage between language and experience.

In the model we are presenting, rather than predeciding

on a specific number and description of parts, we use an n-parts model. This n-parts model gives the therapist more flexibility than that of using a model with a predetermined number and description of parts. By n-parts model we mean that there can be any number of parts and when using this n-parts model we generally label the part by function and get a direct behavioral description via the 5 tuple.

19

CONGRUITY VS. INCONGRUITY

All behavior is communication about the internal organization of an individual. Communication is carried out
through many channels; these channels are both verbal
(words) and non-verbal (analogical behavior). When all communication channels are carrying messages that match, it is
referred to as congruity. In some situations, the multiple
channels of information offered carry mismatched messages,
that is, messages which offer conflicting data. When the information offered by an individual does not match or conflicts,
it is referred to as incongruity.

One way to organize the many channels of communication which exist in human beings is verbal versus non-verbal.
In many schools of thought it is believed that the real or true
message is carried by non-verbal channels, however, it is our
belief that all messages offered are valid and real messages.
Since all behavior is communication, in the case of a client
who is communicating incongruently, it is safe to assume that
within the whole person there are conflicting parts concerning a certain content area. One could easily say that there is

more than one map for the same territory. We refer to each of these messages as paramessages. Below is a list of verbal and non-verbal communication channels.

Verbal	Non-Verbal
Words	Body Posture
	Voice Tone
	Voice Tempo
	Breathing Rate
	Gestures
	Eye Movements

	Verbal	Non-Verbal
Client:	I really love my wife.	(Head shaking back and forth, voice tone loud and harsh, fists clenched tightly.)
	* * *	
Client:	I'm so angry at Terry.	(Voice tone quiet and soft, breathing rate slow and even.)

In both of these examples the verbal portions of communication conflict with the non-verbal portions. The observant therapist would notice this incongruity and realize that there are two conflicting maps existing for each client. When conflicting messages are offered at the same time it is referred to as simultaneous incongruency.

In some cases, the conflicting messages are communicated one after the other in sequence. This is referred to as sequential incongruency.

Example:

I love my wife, however, at times she really angers me.

Paramessage
1. I really love my wife.
2. At times she angers me.

* * *

Example:

I'm so angry at Nick, but at times he really is a lovable guy.

Paramessage
1. I'm angry at Nick.
2. Nick is a lovable guy.

In the case of sequential incongruity, each of the paramessages may be simultaneously congruent or incongruent:

Verbal	**Non-Verbal**
The kids are a real pleasure.	(Smile on face, even breathing rate, soft steady voice tone/tempo, head nodding up and down.)
But at times they drive me nuts.	(Voice tempo even and steady, voice tone soft, head shaking back and forth.)

In the above example, the first paramessage offered is simultaneously congruent, however, the second paramessage offers conflicting data between verbal and non-verbal communication channels.

Hemispheric functioning has an effect on congruency in communication. In many cases, the paramessages carried by the verbal portions of communication and the paramessages carried by the right side of the body will match while the information communicated by the left half of the body will conflict. This is due to the fact that the right side of the body is controlled by the left hemisphere of the brain and it is the left hemisphere or dominant hemisphere which controls verbal communication. The left side of the body is controlled by the non-dominate hemisphere.

Dominant Hemisphere	Non-Dominant Hemisphere
Full Language	Simple Language
Tempo, Grammar, Syntax	Melody, Tonal
Logical	Synthetic, Metaphorical
Abstract	Intuitive, Creative,
Analytical	Spontaneous
	Literal
	Mental Imagery, Spatial
	Relationships
	Kinesthetic[26]

The incongruity which at times exist between the left and right side of the brain is referred to as bilateral incongruency. The generalization concerning hemisphere lateralization holds true for most right handed people; however, there may be some differences in this generalization in the case of left handers.

Sequential incongruencies can be coded in different representational systems and in such cases, one paramessage may presuppose one representational system, while another paramessage presupposes a different representational system.

Example:

I see myself wanting to find a new job, but I feel that it's too scary to try something new.

Paramessage
1. I see myself wanting to find a new job (Visual).

2. feel too scary to try something new (Kinesthetic).

* * *

Example:

Going to Florida sounds great to me. However, I can't see myself spending the money.

Paramessage
1. Going to Florida sounds great to me (Auditory).
2. I can't see myself spending the money (Visual).

There are times when one part of the sequential incongruity is expressed verbally and the second part is not expressed. In such cases, the information not expressed is part of the client's subjective experience either conscious or unconscious, and may be available to the client as internal dialogue or via accessing cues.

The therapist can become attuned to this type of incongruency by paying special attention to the endings of the client's sentences. When only a portion of the incongruency is being expressed verbally, the client's voice tone will not drop at the end of the sentence as it usually does when a person ends a sentence. If the therapist inserts the word "but" or "however" at the end of the client's statement, the client will frequently verbalize the other side of the incongruency.

Example:

Client: I really enjoy   (Voice tone does not drop at
               travelling   the end of the sentence.)

Therapist: But?

Client: I hate to pack.

                        *   *   *

Example:

Client: I would love   (Voice tone does not drop at
                 to have a dog   the end of the sentence.)

Therapist: However?

Client: They are too much work.

TAG QUESTIONS

A linguistic pattern found in the work of Milton Erickson, which allows a therapist to pace each side of an incongruency whether it be one directly observable in the client's behavior or one presupposed by the situation, is tag questions. Tag questions, by the very nature of transderivational search in human language, give the therapist direct access to both sides of the incongruency in sequential order. In fact, when utilizing tag questions, if the therapist is selective in using variations of voice tone and tempo, the variations occurring in the first half and the second half of the tag question will themselves act as separate anchors for each portion of the incongruency. It is important, when using tag questions, to keep in mind that words in natural language systems function as an intricate set of anchors.

Example:

You really love your husband (pause), don't you?

It's important to be responsible at work (pause), isn't it?

                  *   *   *

You can change your mind (pause), can't you?

INTEGRATING INCONGRUENCY

In the case of incongruencies, the client has two conflicting maps for the same territory. The client's behavioral and psychological choices are limited to either of these maps, therefore, the client could be considered to be in a philosophical dilemma. The dilemma being that of not having a vast number of choices or options, but instead having to choose one of the two maps. Since it is our presupposition that choices are limited not by the world itself, but by individual models of the world, it is the task of the therapist when working with incongruent behavior to not only give the client the choice of either of the maps but also the range of choices in between. The meta-technique involved in working with incongruency is that of first sorting simultaneous incongruency into sequential incongruency and secondly integrating the sequential incongruency. When the incongruency involved is already a sequential incongruency, the therapist can eliminate the first step.

Exaggeration

The therapist can begin to polarize conflicting maps by taking either side of the incongruency and grossly exaggerating it. The use of gross exaggeration will generally force the client into polarizing one or the other incongruent behavior.

Example:

Client:	I really like my job.	(Client's head nods back and forth.)

Therapist:		(Notices incongruity.)
Therapist:	I'll bet that you just love that job and it's the best job you could ever hope for.	(Therapist uses exaggeration in order to elicit the polarity.)
Client:	Well, in fact, the hours are too long and I'm underpaid.	

Double Chair

Another useful way of systematically polarizing incongruent behavior into sequences is by use of the gestalt technique known as the double chair. When utilizing the double chair the therapist assists the client in sorting each portion of the incongruency, via spacial dislocation, into two empty chairs. This is accomplished by having the client sit in one of the chairs and express one side of the incongruency; the therapist then has the client take the opposite chair and express the other side of the incongruency. This can be done several times by having the client switch back and forth from chair to chair until each portion of the incongruency is fully expressed.

One way to conceptualize the use of the empty chair and spacial dislocation is that each of the chairs, and/or their locations in space are actually anchors. Once both sides of the incongruency has been adequately expressed, the therapist can then assist the client in integrating the incongruency by having him pick up the imagined part, which is sitting in the opposite chair, and pull that part into his chest. This exercise will integrate the incongruent behavior. Integrating incongruencies via double chair could be conceptualized as collapsing anchors; that is, forcing two conflicting neurological patterns into the same time/space coordinates.

Transcript

Client: I really enjoy my job.

Therapist: But?

Client: I feel inadequate in my position.

Therapist: Speak for the part of you that enjoys your job. Start with "I am the part that enjoys my job."

Client: I am the part that enjoys my job and the people I work with. I make good money and I like my hours.

Therapist: Now, please sit in that empty chair and be the part that feels inadequate in your position.

Client: I am the part that feels inadequate in my position because I don't think I can handle the additional responsibility. At times the pressure is just too much, like I can't take any more.

Therapist: Now, see the part of you that really enjoys your job in that empty chair. Reach out with both hands and pick that part up and pull it into your chest.

(Pause)

Client: I guess that there are ways of not taking on so
much work and yet doing a good job.

Visual Squash

Another technique for integrating incongruencies is
known as the visual squash. The therapist, when using the
visual squash, assists the client in sorting the incongruency by
having him see himself in his left hand, expressing one side of
the incongruency, and then see himself in his right hand, expressing the other side. Once the visual image is secured for
both sides of the incongruency, the therapist assists the client
in expanding each image to include the auditory and kinesthetic portions of experience by using overlap of representational systems. Once accomplished, the client will have in
each hand a visual, auditory and kinesthetic experience for
each side of the incongruency. The next step is to have the
client begin to move his hands together until they meet. Once
the hands meet, the two images, with accompanying sounds
and feelings, merge into one image. The client then pulls the
image into his chest and an integration occurs.

Transcript

The client is a 42-year old male who is employed as a professional football coach. The client came into this session
wanting as a goal more options in working with his team, particularly in the area of improved morale and communication.

Client: Well, it's sort of like this. I know it's really
important for me to be assertive and forceful
with the team so they will do what they need
to do as far as training and learning the plays.
However, on the other hand, I have to be nice
enough to these guys so that they like me and
are willing to play as a team for me.

Therapist: Okay, Coach. In your left hand I want you to see yourself as the strong, assertive coach that takes control of the team and gets the job done. Once you have a clear image of yourself then notice the voice tone and the appropriate feelings associated with that image.

Client: (After a few minutes) Okay. I have it.

Therapist: Now, in the other hand see yourself as being supportive, friendly, and easy to get along with. Again, once you have that picture clearly focused then notice the voice tone and feelings associated with that image.

Client: (After a few mintues) Okay.

Therapist: Now, with both hands outstretched, take a moment and concentrate on the images in each hand.

Client: Okay.

Therapist: And now, begin to slowly bring your two hands together, and, once they meet, allow those two images to melt into one.

Client: (After a few minutes) Okay. I have the one image.

Therapist: As you look at this new image and hear the new voice tone you can learn something special . . . and now begin to pull that image into your chest. And, as this new image enters into your chest, notice that special feeling.

Client: (After a few mintues) Okay. I really feel as
though I have more options in working with
my players.

Another variation on the visual squash is to have the client
see the space between his hands as consisting of many visual
slides; as in motion picture film. This will not only be a useful step before the integration occurs but may also give the
client insight into many variations of behavior that exist between the two sides of the incongruency. The integration is
accomplished using this technique in the same way as in the
aforementioned visual squash.

The meta-technique which underlies all of our work is
pacing and leading. If the client is unable to start with the
visual system, the therapist can pace him by beginning with
whichever system is in consciousness. By using overlap of
representational systems, the therapist then expands into
other parameters of experience in order to build a full
representation.

COLLAPSING INCONGRUENCIES

Incongruencies can be integrated quite easily by establishing an anchor for each side of the incongruency and collapsing them. By collapsing of anchors, we mean taking two
established anchors and firing them off simultaneously. This
forces each of the experiences anchored, which were formerly
existing in separate time/space coordinates, to now occupy
the same time and space. Conflicting neurological maps cannot exist in the same time/space coordinates without
integrating.

Transcript

Therapist: What specific change would you like for yourself today?

Client: I would like to stop worrying all the time.

Therapist: You mean you worry all the time?

Client: No, not all the time, but I do find that I
worry about situations and later realize that
I did all the worrying for nothing.

Therapist: What specific situations do you worry about?

Client: When I'm driving in my car, I worry about
getting into an accident.

Therapist: How would you like to feel while you're
driving?

Client: Well, I would like to relax and enjoy the
drive, but I really feel that if I'm not on my
toes and very careful, I'll get in an accident.

Therapist: Do you often get into accidents?

Client: No, in fact, I've never even gotten a ticket.

Therapist: Get in touch with the part of you that feels
comfortable and calm, and once you have
contacted that part, allow those feelings to
intensify.

Client: Okay.

Therapist: (Notices minimal cues of decreased breathing rate, paling of the skin and relaxation of muscle tension of the face and arms. Therapist establishes anchor on the right wrist.)

Therapist: Now, take a moment and clear consciousness.

Client: Alright.

Therapist: Now, get in touch with the part of you responsible for the worrying, and become immersed in those feelings.

Client: I'll try.

Therapist: (Notices minimal cues of increased breathing rate, tightening of muscle tension in face and arms and slight flushing of the face. Therapist establishes anchor on the left wrist.)

Therapist: Now clear consciousness.

             (Pause)

Therapist: (Reaches out and fires anchors by touching client on both wrists simultaneously.)

             (After a couple of minutes.)

Therapist: (Notices that integrating has taken place by observing minimal cues; flushing around neck and collar bone, smoothening of facial muscles starting at the ears and moving towards the front of the face.)

Therapist: Take a minute now and imagine yourself driving your car, and tell me how you feel.

(Pause)

Client: I was able to remain comfortable and at the same time confident of my driving skills.

Note: Change was verified at the following session. Client still feels comfortable and confident while driving.

20

RESISTANCE

Resistance is a special case of incongruency. When a client enters treatment there is a presupposed incongruency. This incongruency is that one part of the client wants to change and that part brought the client in for treatment, however, there is another part which has an investment in not changing. It is that part which has stopped the client from already making the desired changes.

Resistance is an important part of treatment and the resistant behavior like all behavior is communication about the internal organization of each client. Once the therapist is able to recognize resistance, the choices are to fight the resistance, or to flow with it. In those cases, when the therapist chooses to fight the resistance, a stronger case of resistance occurs by polarizing the behavior.

From a linguistic point of view, the very act of labeling resistance changes the on-going process of resisting into a static object. The therapist can gather much more information about the behavior by treating the labeled resistance like any other nominalization; that is, by changing it back into a process and recovering the deleted material. The deleted material can be recovered by gathering information around the following questions.

> What specifically is the client resisting?
> How specifically is the client resisting?
> When is the client resisting?
> In what context(s) is the client resisting?

In order to be an effective clinician, it is important to pace the client's resistant behavior. By pacing the resistance, the therapist establishes rapport and, with rapport built, can then work from within the client's model of the world to implement change.

Much of the work done to date on resistance comes from the field of hypnosis, in particular the work of Milton Erickson. Erickson was famous for accepting resistant behavior and utilizing that behavior to assist his clients in changing. Erickson, when faced with a client who believed himself to be Jesus Christ, paced the client by saying: "I understand you are a carpenter." Erickson then proceeded to assign the client tasks that presupposed the skills of carpentry and, finally, put the delusion to work, hammering and sawing. Erickson used the client's own energy in order to implement positive change by rechanneling the behavior.

Another technique for working with resistance is to establish rapport and then integrate the conflicting parts. This may be done by using any of the techniques described in the preceding section on Congruity Vs. Incongruity. In any case, whether utilizing resistance or integrating the resistant parts, secondary gains are often an integral part of resistance. The therapist can begin exploring these secondary gains by examining what positive function the resistance serves in the client's life and exploring alternative means of satisfying this positive function. Secondary gains will be discussed in greater detail in the section on Reframing.

The Zen Master and The Priest

One day there was a Zen master talking to a group of students about the teachings of Zen. In the audience there was a priest who stood and said, "Since I don't believe in Zen, you cannot teach me anything." The Zen master responded by saying, "Please, come up onto the stage with me so we can discuss this issue." The priest gladly agreed and came forward to talk with the master. After conversing for a while, the Zen master said "Let's go to the back of the stage and sit at the table", to which the priest complied. As they continued their discussion, the Zen master suggested to the priest what a fine day it was for walking and enjoying nature in the woods. Soon, the priest led the way as he and the Zen master strolled together in the woods. After a time, the Zen master pointed to a spot under a tree where they could sit, and there they sat, discussing further the value of the teachings of Zen.

Paraphrased from "Zen Flesh Zen Bones."

21

TIME ORIENTATION

A factor in the design of a treatment strategy is how a person is oriented in time. For the purpose of clinical application we will take the ongoing continuum of time and divide it into three categories; past, present and future. Clients use time as a reference system and within the realm of subjective experience shift their conscious awareness to one of the three time orientations.

PAST ORIENTATION

In the case of past oriented clients, their language is often indicative of past events and memories. Many times these memories are exact representations of the perceptions of events as they actually occurred; however, in some cases, these memories have been altered by adding to or subtracting from the experience. These memories are indeed maps of past experiences and therefore are subject to the operations of distortion, deletion and generalization.

A past oriented client may effectively use this orientation as a valuable resource in being able to learn and grow from past experiences. On the other hand, a past oriented client may find himself being overwhelmed by feelings from the past and/or getting lost in daydreaming about past events. For some individuals, dwelling on the past becomes an obsession which occupies much of their time, excluding planning for the future and living in the here and now.

FUTURE ORIENTATION

Future oriented clients are those who spend the bulk of their time thinking about future plans and dreams. These individuals will frequently speak about what they will do tomorrow, next week or next year. The realm of this time orientation is largely that of fantasy and imagination.

The future orientation can be a useful tool in creativity and planning for tomorrow. The work of architects, engineers and artists comes from the effective use of the future time orientation. In the process of goal setting the future orientation can be used via imagining where you want to be and what you would like to be doing.

A future time orientation can also be a source of limitations; such as, the client who lives in a world of dreaming about tomorrow and doing nothing today to make it happen. In some cases, this orientation lends itself to the starry-eyed dreamer who shuns reality for pleasant fantasy. There are also those individuals who use this ability to project their subjective experience into the future as a way to create worry for themselves, imagining the worst and feeling as though it has happened.

PRESENT ORIENTATION

One could define the present strictly as being sensory experience or uptime (V^e, A^e, K^e, O^e, G^e), however, for practical purposes, we prefer to use a looser definition which includes both sensory experience and internal experience (thinking). The internal experience generally involved in present time orientation is the manipulation of factors in sensory experience so as to problem solve; such as, a client working on a jigsaw puzzle. By staying in the here and now, the client is solving the task before him and in the process of solving the puzzle, he is not only aware of seeing the pieces in front of him, hearing them as they touch, and feeling them in his fingers, but in his mind he is manipulating the pieces visually in order to search for possible solutions.

The client who is primarily in present time orientation will tend to talk about what is going on in the here and now, while making little reference to the past or future. This client can use the present as a resource in the sense of dealing with the here and now, without worrying about the future or obsessing over the past. The possible limitations to this orientation are that a present oriented individual may not plan for the future or learn from his mistakes. Should this be the case, the present time orientation would serve as a handicap.

PRIMARY TIME ORIENTATION

Much like in the case of representational systems, each client at times uses past, present, and future time orientations to accomplish the tasks of day-to-day living, however, most clients have a preference for one of the orientations. We refer to the most highly valued or preferred time orientations as primary time orientation (P.T.O.). One of the easiest ways of detecting a client's primary time orientation is by listening to the sentences generated and determining whether the verbs are past, present or future tense. A generalization which holds true in determining a client's primary time orientation is that past oriented clients tend to use accessing cues which presuppose the non-dominant hemisphere, (V^r, A^r, K^r, O^r, G^r) while future oriented clients use accessing cues which presuppose the dominant hemisphere (V^c, A^c, K^c, O^c, G^c). By observing accessing cues, the therapist can determine, via hemispheric functioning, a client's P.T.O. To make an accurate evaluation it is helpful for the therapist to use both accessing cues and verb tense.

Once the therapist has determined the client's primary time orientation, rapport is established by pacing the preferred orientation. When pacing, the therapist speaks about content areas which presupposes the client's P.T.O. In addition to this, the therapist can match verb tense and even mirror the appropriate accessing cues. As in all pacing, the purpose of this initial step is to build rapport which can later be used as a spring board for change. Since our basic presupposition in therapy is that choice is better than no choice, it is our task to assist clients in increasing their options by having them effectively utilize all three time orientations. Along with the ability to have the fluidity in subjective experience to shift consciousness from one orientation to another, we also work to assist the client in making the best choice as to the suitability of each time orientation for the desired task.

Much like overlapping representational systems, the therapist, once having established a pace via time orientation, can begin to expand on the client's time orientation by overlapping from that state of consciousness to one which presupposes a different orientation.

Transcript:

Client: I really feel bad about my recent divorce.

Therapist: How long has it been since your divorce?

Client: Three years, but it still feels like it was just
               yesterday. You know, I have tried to get on
               with my life, however, I find myself sitting
               around the house lost in memories.

Note   (Client has a past P.T.O. and appears unable
               to utilize the present and/or future orienta-
               tions.)

Therapist: I 'elieve I understand how you feel. Let's
               take a minute and really get in touch with
               those memories.

Client: Okay.

               (Pause)

Therapist: Now, can we set those memories aside for just
               a few minutes and begin to slowly focus our
               attention into the future?

Client: Okay.

Therapist: For just a moment, I would like you to look
               up and begin to see yourself six months from
               now and as you do that, focus clearly on
               those situations in the future which will allow
               you to be happy.

               (Pause)

Client: Okay, I've got two pictures.

Therapist: What's going on in those pictures?

Client: Well, in one, I see myself playing golf again and in the other I see myself driving a sports car.

Therapist: As you see those images of the future, put yourself into each of those scenes and then notice your feelings.

(Pause)

Therapist: How do you feel?

Client: In both scenes I felt really good.

Note (The therapist has successfully led the client from a past P.T.O. into utilizing a future time orientation in order to set goals.)

Therapist: What can you do now that will allow you to work towards achieving those goals?

Client: Well, the guy at the office has been asking me to play golf. I will take him up on his offer.

Therapist: How realistic is having a sports car?

Client: I can afford one and it would be fun. All I have to do is start shopping around.

Note (The therapist, once establishing goals by using future time orientation, leads the client to the present time orientation in order to begin the step by step process of making the goals possible.)

We have found that once we begin to teach clients, by overlap of time orientation, to shift their consciousness among the three orientations, that this skill begins to generalize to many areas of their lives. This ability to shift consciousness not only gives a client more options, but in most cases, access to resources stored in the past, present and/or future.

PART III

The patient needs an experience,
not an explanation.

Frieda Fromm-Reichmann

22

TECHNIQUES
OF CHANGE

This section of our text is dedicated to presenting a number of psychotherapeutic techniques designed to assist clients in achieving their goals. All of the techniques presented in this section presuppose the use of anchoring as a mechanism to stabilize states of consciousness, resources and contexts. As we present each of the techniques, we will indicate which problems they work best in solving and which clients they might best be suited in treating.

COLLAPSING ANCHORS

Collapsing anchors is the process whereby two experiences formerly occupying different time/space coordinates are integrated together so as to occupy the same time and space. Conflicting neurological patterns which are forced into the same time/space coordinates will integrate and the integration which occurs allows the individual not only the choices offered by either of the conflicting patterns but, in addition, the entire range of choices existing in-between. A therapist can easily work with a client utilizing the technique of collapsing anchors by eliciting two states of consciousness, establishing a separate anchor for each experience, and then integrating the experiences by firing off both anchors simultaneously. In order for the anchors to integrate completely the experiences anchored must be of approximately the same intensity and the anchors must be held for a few moments until an integration begins. Collapsing anchors is a useful tool in integrating sequential incongruence (see page 120), however, it is also an effective technique when working with a client who has two or more disassociated states of consciousness with no connecting bridges. A good example of disassociated states is that of alcoholism.

An alcoholic client has certain resources and limitations in both the sober and intoxicated states of consciousness, however, these two states of consciousness are so severely disassociated that a drug (alcohol) is needed to get from one state to the other. In order for an alcoholic to change into a well integrated human being, the therapist must assist the client in bringing the two dissociated states of consciousness together by integrating them. There are many theories on alcoholism which do not work to integrate these disassociated states and the outcome is that of producing a situation in which the client has the choice to drink or avoid drinking. These clients seem to be constantly in the midst of an internal battle between these two choices and each choice is a metaphoric way of representing a part of their own internal make-up. It is no wonder that many clients, victims of a non-integrative model of therapy, spend their lives in constant conflict, either drinking or fighting not to drink. It is our belief that the resources available to the client in each of the states of consciousness (sober and intoxicated) are valuable parts of the client's personality and each of these states have within their parameters, resources needed for the client to be a well integrated person.

When working with an alcoholic client, the therapist must first gain access to and then establish a separate anchor for both states of consciousness. With both anchors well established, the therapist collapses the anchors in order to produce an integration. In many cases, this integration takes several minutes and produces a profoundly altered state of consciousness. This altered state is the product of having two states of consciousness, which have been disassociated for years, come together. Collapsing anchors, in itself, will not "cure" the alcoholic; however, it is a good start in the direction of recovery. In order to get long-term change, it is important to deal with the secondary gains both in the client and in the family system. We frequently work with this issue utilizing a technique called reframing, which will be described later in this volume.

Transcript

Therapist: What specific change do you want for yourself today?

Client: I want to quit drinking alcohol.

Therapist: What would being sober do for you?

Client: I would stop getting into trouble.

Therapist: What kind of trouble do you get into?

Client: I have three drunk driving convictions and I have been caught drinking on the job.

Therapist: Anything else?

Client: My wife, she says that if I don't get some help and quit drinking, she will divorce me.

Therapist: Why would she do that?

Client: Well, when I get drunk, I get very angry and start yelling, screaming, and throwing things around.

Therapist: Do you get angry when you are sober?

Client: No, I'm real shy, quiet and calm but, when I drink, I don't know, I just get mad.

Therapist: Okay. Now let me get this straight, you want to quit drinking alcohol completely?

Client: That's right.

Therapist: How much and how often do you drink?

Client: I drink two to three times per week and about one pint of whiskey each time.

Therapist: Do you use any other drugs or take any medication?

Client: No.

Therapist: Now, let's go back a way. What will not drinking do for you except help you stay out of trouble and keep your marriage together?

Client: I would feel better about myself. When I get in trouble and get angry I feel guilty and bad the next couple of days.

Therapist: Now, what I want you to do is take a moment and remember what it's like to be intoxicated.

Once you can remember allow yourself to feel intoxicated and immerse yourself in the state of drunkeness.

(Pause)

Client: Okay, I can feel my body beginning to get high.

Therapist: Good, close your eyes, and remember the smell of whiskey and really feel drunk.

Client: You know that judge has a lot of nerve taking away my license.

(Words slur, skin reddens deeply, voice is loud as breathing rate increases)

Therapist: (Reaches over and gently touches client on the right wrist to anchor intoxicated state)

Therapist: Okay. Now, begin to come back to this room leaving those feelings behind as you gently sober up.

(A couple of minutes pass)

Client: (Opens eyes)

You know I really felt drunk.

(Words no longer slurred, voice tone calm, skin slightly flushed, breathing rate slower)

But, I feel sober as a judge now.

Therapist: Now, what's being sober like for you?

Client: I feel calm, relaxed, quiet.

Therapist: (Therapist reaches over and gently touches client on the left wrist to anchor sober state)

(A couple of minutes pass)

(Therapist reaches over and fires anchor for the intoxicated state by touching client's right wrist. Therapist notices skin color reddens, breathing rate increases)

Client: When you touch my wrist I start feeling drunk.

(Speech is slightly slurred)

Therapist: That's okay.

(A few minutes pass)

Now you know what those two states are for you, sobriety and drunkeness, don't you?

Client: Yes.

Therapist: (Therapist reaches over and fires both anchors by touching the client's left and right wrists simultaneously for a few minutes)

Client: (Client at first seems to vacillate from one state of consciousness to the other, back and forth; however, after a couple of minutes the anchors begin to integrate)

Therapist: (Therapist notices the integration occurring
                  by seeing the muscle tone smoothening, start-
                  ing at the ears and moving towards the front
                  of the face)

                  As you become aware of those sensations,
                  you may find that new ways of satisfying old
                  needs are becoming available to you.

                  (Therapist lets up on the anchors and sits
                  back, waiting for the integration to be com-
                  pleted, about three minutes)

In the aforementioned transcript, the therapist was careful to elicit a good representation of the client's intoxicated
state and to do so he employed the olfactory sense, the smell
of whiskey. The olfactory sense has direct cortical projec-
tion which allows for quick time/space disassociation, thereby facilitating easy access to past memories of intoxication.
The therapist also notices behavioral signs of intoxication,
flushing of skin and slurring of words along with angry voice
tone which was described by the client as an emotion frequently available during drinking behavior.

Collapsing anchors is an excellent tool in integrating disassociated states of consciousness. In the transcript provided,
alcoholism was the presenting problem, however, this technique is equally applicable to other compulsive behavior,
such as   overeating, smoking, drug abuse and nail biting.

Algorithm for Integrating Discrete States of Consciousness

1. Elicit each state of consciousness and establish a separate
   anchor for each state.

2. Verify that each anchor is firmly established.

3. Fire off both anchors simultaneously.

4. Verify (via sensory experience) that an integration has occurred.

COLLAPSING ANCHORS FOR INTEGRATIVE EDUCATION

Collapsing anchors is an excellent tool for integrating two or more bodies of information or systems of knowledge. When utilizing collapsing anchors for this purpose, the therapist elicits from the client experiences which are representative of each content distinction, establishes an anchor for each and integrates the anchors. When eliciting the representation for each body of knowledge, it is important that the representation include all parameters of the five tuple. These representations are metaphors for the entire system of thought.

We have found that collapsing anchors is a technique particularly useful in conducting workshops and in training therapists. In many cases, when people learn new information they are able to master the knowledge. However, this knowledge and any pre-existing knowledge exists in mutually exclusive categories and, as such, they can operate out of either one or the other system but not any combination of the two systems. In this case, collapsing anchors can help facilitate a melting of the two or more previously mutually exclusive categories. As we have stated numerous times throughout this text, the object is to increase choices; having options available from both systems of knowledge generally increases choices.

It is important to address the issue of integrating knowledge versus translating knowledge. We believe that the integration of knowledge vastly improves effectiveness and choices, however, some people insist on taking new knowledge and translating it into terms, categories, and theories which previously existed for them. This translation, we believe, does a great disservice to the learner because it inhibits the learning of anything new. Instead of acquiring new knowledge and the subtle nuances involved in this knowledge, the process of merely shuffling the knowledge into old categories both makes the new old and, in many cases, loses the subtleties involved.

Transcript

Kim: What specific change do you want for yourself today?

Participant: I have been a T.A. therapist for a number of years and I believed that I had learned a lot about N.L.P., however, I don't seem to be able to integrate the two models.

Kim: Fine. I would like you to take a moment, close your eyes and make an internal representation of your understanding of T.A., make sure that this representation includes visual, auditory, and kinesthetic parameters of experience and if any smells or tastes are associated with that model include them also.

                (A few minutes pass)

Participant: Okay, I've got it.

Kim: (Notices a slight flushing of the skin and reaches over to touch the participant on the left knee in order to anchor that experience)

                Now, come back to the here and now.

Participant: That was interesting.

Kim: (Reaches over and touches participant's left knee to verify anchor. Kim notices the slight flushing of skin associated with that state of consciousness)

                Now, go inside and make a representation of your knowledge of N.L.P., again being sure that all parameters of the 5-tuple are represented.

                (A few minutes pass)

Participant: Okay, I have it.

Kim: (Notices a lowering of the left eye brow; reaches over and touches participant on the right knee to anchor that experience)

                Now, clear consciousness and come back to this room.

Participant: That was a real different experience.

Kim: (Tests anchor by touching participant's right knee and notices a lowering of the left eye brow)

                Now, the next step will be to integrate these two experiences.

                (Reaches over and collapses anchors by touching both knees simultaneously)

                (A couple of minutes pass)

(Notices that an integration is occurring by the smoothening of facial muscles and a slight flushing at the neck)

(Anchors the integration by touching the client's right shoulder while the integration is coming to a peak)

Participant: That is a strange sensation.

Kim: Where do you want this new integration to be most readily available to you?

Participant: In my office.

Kim: Take a moment and imagine that you are in your office.

(Pause)

Participant: Okay.

Kim: (Reaches over and touches participant's right shoulder firing off the anchor for the integration. A slight flushing of the neck begins to occur)

(Pause)

Take a moment and imagine yourself working with a client.

Participant: Okay.

(A few minutes pass)

Kim: How did it go? Were you able to use this new
                  integration?

Participant: Yes, it was great. I was able to use skills from
                  T.A. and N.L.P.

Kim: Good. Is there anything else you want today?

Participant: No, thank you.

Algorithm for Integrating Learning Systems

1. Elicit a metaphoric representation which includes all parameters of the 5-tuple for each learning system.

2. Establish a separate anchor for each system.

3. Verify that each anchor is established.

4. Fire off the anchors simultaneously.

5. Verify that an integration is occurring.

6. While integration is at its peak establish an anchor for the integration.

7. Future pace the integration.

8. Verify the future pace by having the client go through the situation where the integration is desired without using the anchors.

CREATING EXPERIENCE

Collapsing anchors can be utilized both as a tool of remedial change and as a tool with application in the area of generative personality. With remedial application, the goal is to assist a client in solving or fixing problems, whereas, in generative change, the challenge is that of creating new experiences. For many years generative change was referred to as personal growth. Thus far in this section, we have discussed ways in which collapsing anchors can be used to integrate experiences which are fragmented or in some cases, disassociated. Collapsing anchors, however, can just as easily and, in some cases more interestingly, be used to create a whole new world of experience.

Collapsing anchors, when utilized to create generative change, assists the client in blending experiences that have within them positive and creative resources. The blending of these experiences not only creates new experiences but also, new resources. There are numerous methods for gaining access to resources, however, collapsing anchors allows for the creation of new resources which are the by-product of bringing together pre-existing experiences.

Transcript

The following transcript is taken from a two-day workshop.

Kim: Who would like to have the opportunity to explore some new experiences?

(A man in the audience volunteers to participate in the demonstration. The participant comes to the front of the room and sits on the chair)

All that we are going to do is to play with the idea of anchoring in such a way as to create some new experiences.

Participant: Fine.

Kim: I wonder if you could choose two of the most delightful and creative aspects of your personality. Let me assure you that what we will do here will in no way limit your ability to have and use those parts of you, however, I will assist you in adding an additional choice, a new part. Now take a moment and choose two parts.

(A few minutes pass)

Participant: I have them.

Kim: Fine, can you give me a word for each?

Participant: Creativity and strength.

Kim: I would like you to take a moment, go inside and experience creativity. Notice how it feels to be creative and pay attention to any visual images and sounds which are associated with creativity.

(Pause)

(Notices a slight flushing of the face and a deepening of breathing in the participant. As the experience appears to peak, Kim reaches over and anchors it by touching the participant on the right shoulder)

Now take a moment, clear consciousness, and once you have done so, go inside and find an experience which best represents you as a person with strength.

(A few moments pass)

Participant: Okay, I have it.

Kim: (Noticing that the experience of strength is peaking, reaches over and touches the participant on his right wrist in order to anchor the experience)

(Pause)

Kim: Now, clear consciousness.

(Pause)

Participant: Okay.

Kim: (Reaches over and touches the participant's right shoulder and notices response, "creativity," re-elicited)

(After a few moments pass, Kim reaches over and touches the participant's right wrist and notices that response, "strength" is re-elicited)

Now, let's go for something new.

(Reaches over and touches the participant's right shoulder and right wrist simultaneously, collapsing anchors)

Participant: (Shifts back and forth between experience
                creativity and experience strength until an
                integration occurs)

                (A few moments pass)

                Wow, what a trip, that is really weird.

Kim: Now you know that you have one more ex-
                perience which can be utilized as a resource in
                your day-to-day life.

Algorithm for Creating Experience

1. Determine which experiences will be the root of the new
   experiences.

2. Elicit the root experiences.

3. Establish an anchor for each root experience.

4. Verify that each anchor is established.

5. Integrate the root experiences by collapsing anchors.

BRIEF THERAPY

The brief therapy paradigm is one that utilizes anchoring
to systematically unite a resource with the context in which
the resource is needed.[27] In this paradigm, the therapist
establishes an anchor for the context in which the client
wants to make a change. Usually this context is an example
of a general class of contexts; by this we mean that many
people come into therapy because they experience a problem
which occurs time and time again. In many cases, this pro-

blem occurs in very similar, although at times, not identical contexts.

Once the therapist has stabilized the context through anchoring, the next step is to determine what resource(s) is needed in order to make the change necessary for client goal achievement. After the resource(s) needed has been determined, the therapist assists the client in gaining access to the desired resource(s) by searching the client's personal history for a time and/or context when the resource was available. As the client experiences the desired resource, the therapist skillfully anchors the resource and then verifies that the anchors for both context and resource are installed. Since an anchor has been established for both the resource and the context; by collapsing the anchors the resource will become integrated into the context. Finally, to ensure that the new resource continues to be available in the desired context or general class of contexts, the therapist future paces the new resource. The future pacing step is accomplished by anchoring the resource to a naturally occurring indicator which allows the client to know that he is in that general class of contexts. The indicator can be elicited by simply asking the client How do you know that you are in the context where you want the desired resource? The verbal and/or non-verbal response to this question will supply the therapist with the indicator. The resource is then anchored to the indicator.

The brief therapy paradigm is most effective with present and/or future oriented clients. This technique is designed for a change in the here and now which is then projected into the future. We have found that for a client who insists upon bringing up the past, this technique does not always adequately pace his model of the world.

Transcript

Therapist: What specific change would you like for yourself today?

Client: (Eyes shift up and to the left, V^r and then down and to the right, K^i)

I feel very anxious over my poor performance in my speech class. It seems

(Eyes shift up and to the left, V^r)

every time I get up in front of the class to give a speech I

(Eyes shift down and to the right, K^i) ·

freeze.

Therapist: What is the experience of freezing like for you?

Client: (Eyes shift down and to the right, K^i)

I just get overwhelmed with fear.

Therapist: So my understanding is that you would like to function differently when giving a speech. Now, how specifically would you like to feel when presenting a speech?

Client: (Eyes shift down and to the right, K^i)

I would like to feel comfortable.

Therapist: How specifically would you know when you're feeling comfortable in that situation?

Client: (Eyes shift down and to the right, K^i)

My stomach would be calm.

Therapist:	Take a moment and go back to the last time you had the experience of feeling overwhelming fear about giving a speech and allow yourself to become immersed in that experience.
Client:	(Closes eyes and becomes immersed in the context.)
	(A few moments pass.)
Therapist:	(Notices that the client's body is becoming tense, lips constrict as skin loses color.)
Therapist:	(Reaches over and touches client on the right knee to anchor that experience.)
Therapist:	Fine, now come back to this room.
Therapist:	(Notices that the client's color returns as his body relaxes.)
Therapist:	Now, what resources would you need in order to feel comfortable when giving a speech?
Client:	(Eyes shift up and to the right, V^c and then down and to the right, K^i)
	I'd need confidence.
Therapist:	Has there ever been a time in your life when you've been confident?
Client:	(Eyes shift up and to the left, V^r and blinks quickly 5 times as if flicking through several pictures and then shifts down and to the right, K^i)

Sure.

Therapist: Good, take a moment and get in touch with that resource and allow yourself to really feel confident.

Client: (Eyes shift up and to the left, V^r and then down and to the right, K^i)

(Pause)

I feel the confidence.

Therapist: (Notices a slight flushing in the client's face and an increase in breathing depth and rate)

Therapist: (Reaches out and touches client on his left knee to anchor the resource confidence)

Therapist: Now, clear consciousness and come back to the here and now.

(Pause)

Therapist: (Fires off each anchor while watching minimal cues in order to test anchors)

(Pause)

Therapist: O.K. Now, let's put the two together. I want you to take a moment and go through the situation of giving a speech, only this time, know that you are doing so with a new resource.

Client: Alright. (Closes eyes)

Therapist: (Fires off both anchors simultaneously by touching both knees and holds anchors down)

               (A few moments pass.)

Therapist: (Notices that the client does not exhibit the minimal cues; body tension, lip constriction and pale skin previously associated with the speech giving experience. Client instead exhibits relaxed muscle tones and a slight flushing of the face.)

Client: (Opens eyes after a few moments)

Therapist: How did it go?

Client: Great.

Therapist: Did you get the outcome that you wanted?

Client: Yes.

Therapist: Now, what is the first thing that you would see, feel or hear to let you know that you are in the speech giving situation?

Client: (Eyes shift up and to the left, V^r)

               I would see the faces of my classmates.

Therapist: Fine. Now, make a picture in your head of your classmates.

Client: (Eyes shift up and to the left, V^r)

Therapist: (As the client's eyes shift up and to the left the therapist touches the client on his left wrist in order to future pace the resource. The future pace step is accomplished by anchoring the needed resource to the client's context indicator.)

(Pause)

Therapist: Now, go through the situation of giving a speech.

(The therapist has client go through the situation of giving a speech in his head without the use of any anchors to verify that the future pacing step has automated the anchoring process.)

Client: (Eyes shift up and to the left, V^r then down and to the right, K^i)

(A few minutes pass.)

Therapist: (Verifies via minimal cues; relaxed muscle tones and slight flushing of facial skin, that the client utilized the resource.)

Therapist: How did it turn out this time?

Client: Fine.

In the aforementioned transcript, the young man came in with an inability to talk in front of his class. The therapy session took approximately twenty minutes. The client came back two weeks later for a follow-up session, stating that he was doing fine in his speech class and felt comfortable and confident giving speeches.

Algorithm for Brief Therapy

1. Determine the context where the change is desired.

2. Establish an anchor for the context.

3. Determine which resource is needed to achieve the desired change.

4. Assist the client in gaining access to the needed resource by having him search his personal history for a time/place when the resource was available.

5. Establish an anchor for the resource.

6. Collapse the anchor for the context and the anchor for the resource by firing them off simultaneously.

7. Verify that the outcome is the desired one, if not return to Step 3 to gather additional resources.

8. Future pace the resource(s) by anchoring the resource(s) to a naturally occurring indicator of the context.

FORM VERSUS CONTENT

In order to fully understand and utilize the approach to therapy described in this volume, an essential distinction to make is that of Form vs. Content. Form or process is the relationship(s) among variable(s). The variables involved may represent specific content distinctions, such as: certain issues in a client's life, specific resources, contexts where change is desired, or entire classes of information (e.g. visual, kinesthetic, auditory, olfactory, gustatory). To use an analogy borrowed from mathematics, let's examine a simple equation.

$$A \rangle B$$

In this equation the symbol $\rangle$ stands for greater than and is a process distinction which describes the relationship between the variables A and B. In the equation there are two variables (A and B) which may stand for specific sets of numbers, e.g., A = [1, 2, 3, 4, 5, 6, 7, 8, 9, 10...] B = [1, 2, 3, 4, 5, 6, 7, 8, 9, 10...] or general classes of information e.g. all integers greater than 0; A $\rangle$ 0, B $\rangle$ 0. Using the same equation one could replace the variables with numbers; 6 $\rangle$ 5 in this case the $\rangle$ sign would still describe the relationship, however, the variables would be replaced by specific content distinctions, 6 and 5 respectively.

A further example illustrating the distinction between form and content is that of examining a simple three point strategy utilizing representational systems.

$$V \to A \to K$$

image of → mother's face	sound of her voice →	feelings of joy
image of → parents' fighting	loud sound of → their voice	feelings of scare
image of → green trees	sound of the → rustling wind	feelings of comfort

In the aforementioned illustration the content of each example varies greatly, however, the form remains the same.

In the V-A-K calculus, each letter (V, A, and K) stands for a general class of information, that is: visual, auditory and kinesthetic. In addition, the order of the variables, V-A-K, indicates the relationship among them. Each of the examples illustrating this strategy has varying content distinctions; however, of primary importance is the constancy of form.

When change is implemented on the formal level the change is more likely to permeate across numerous contexts so as to affect any contexts which belong to the same general class. This type of generalization makes it possible for the client to make a change by working through one specific issue and having that change then affect future situations which are similar to the issue around which the work was done. The study of form deals primarily with the question of "How?" and, to be more specific, this book explores the "How" of change.

CONTENT FREE THERAPY

Much of the work we do is actually formal change which allows us, at times, to do content free therapy. Content free therapy is the ultimate utilization of process oriented therapeutic intervention and permits the therapist to assist in change without needing to know the content issue. The content free paradigm forces the therapist to make therapeutic intervention totally on the formal level. Working on the formal level eliminates the possibility of the therapist becoming active in the content issue, and influencing the client by imposing values. When assisting a client during private counseling sessions, content free therapy is extremely effective. Content free work is also of equal value when working with a volunteer in a seminar setting where the participant might have reservations about verbalizing any therapeutic issues in a public arena.

In order to illustrate the use of content free therapy, the following is a transcript which utilizes the brief therapy paradigm, content free.

Transcript

Linda:	Who has a problem which reoccurs and wants to make a change around that issue?
	(A person raises his hand and walks to the front of the audience.)
Linda:	Now, I don't want you to tell me about your problem. We are going to do content free therapy.
Participant:	Fine
Linda:	There is a change that you want, right?
Participant:	Yes.
Linda:	Could you give that situation or context in which you want the change a code name.
Participant:	Sure, let's call it A.
Linda:	Fine, so you want to make a change in context A?
Participant:	Yes.
Linda:	Okay, take a moment and go back to context A and re-experience it.
Participant:	(Closes his eyes; his muscles begin to tense up and his skin begins to pale.)
Linda:	(Notices that the participant is re-experiencing the problem. Linda reaches over and

touches the participant on the right wrist in order to anchor the experience.)

Linda: Okay. Now, come back to the here and now.

Participant: Okay.

Linda: What resource would you need in order to get the outcome that you want in that situation and give that resource a code name.

Participant: I would need B.

Linda: Can you imagine what it would be like to have B?

Participant: Sure.

Linda: Imagine what it would be like now, and allow yourself to become immersed in B until you experience it.

Participant: Fine.

Participant: (Closes his eyes; muscle tone begins to relax, lip size swells slightly, and skin color flushes considerably.)

Linda: (Reaches over and touches participant on the left forefinger in order to anchor the experience.)

Linda: Now, clear consciousness.

Linda: (Both anchors are tested to ensure that they elicit the appropriate responses which are verified by observing minimal cues.)

Linda: Now, go through situation A with resource B.

Participant: (Closes his eyes and goes through the situation.)

Linda: (As the participant begins to go through the situation, Linda touches the participant on the right wrist and the left forefinger and holds down those two spots in order to collapse the anchors.)

Participant: (At first participant's lips swell slightly, muscle tone relaxes, and skin color flushes; however, after a few moments, participant's muscles begin to tense and flushing begins to leave his face.)

Participant: (Opens his eyes.)

Linda: How did that turn out?

Participant: It was better.

Linda: But . . .

Participant: It wasn't quite right.

Linda: What additional resource would you need and give it a code name.

(Pause)

Participant: Okay, C.

Linda: Have you ever had C?

Participant: Sure.

Linda: Take a moment and re-experience C.

Participant: (Closes his eyes; muscle tone becomes relaxed, lip size swells and skin flushes.)

Linda: (Notices the participant's responses then reaches over and touches the participant's left thumb in order to anchor the experience.)

Participant: (Opens his eyes.)

Linda: (Tests the anchor to ensure that it elicits the appropriate response.)

Linda: Now, go through situation A with resources B and C.

Participant: (Closes his eyes and begins to go through situation A.)

Linda: (Reaches over and fires off the anchors for situation A and resources B and C.)

Participant: (Muscle tone relaxes, lip size swells and skin flushes considerably.)

                  (A few moments pass.)

Linda: How did it turn out?

Participant: Much better.

Linda:	Did you get the outcome that you wanted?
Participant:	Yes.
Linda:	Good. Now, what is the first thing that you would see, feel, or hear that will let you know that you're in situation A.
Participant:	A tight feeling in my chest.
Linda:	Feel that tight feeling, now.
Participant:	Okay, I've got it.
Linda:	(Fires off anchors for B and C by touching the participant's left thumb and left forefinger as he experiences the tight feeling; future pace step.)
	(A moment passes.)
Linda:	Now, once more go through situation A, this time with no anchors.
Participant:	(Closes his eyes. As he goes through situation A his muscle tone becomes relaxed, lip size swells, and skin flushes considerably.)
	(A few moments pass.)
Linda:	Is there anything else you want from this piece of work?
Participant:	No.

Algorithm for Content Free Therapy

1. Determine the context where the change is desired. Establish a code name for that context.

2. Establish an anchor for the context.

3. Determine which resource is needed to achieve the desired change and establish a code name for the resource.

4. Assist the client in gaining access to the needed resource by having him search his personal history for a time/place when/where the resource was available.

5. Establish an anchor for the resource.

6. Verify that both anchors are established by testing them.

7. Collapse the anchor for the context and the anchor for the resource by firing them off simultaneously.

8. Verify that the outcome is the desired one.

9. If the outcome was the one desired move to step 10, if not, backtrack to step 3 in order to gather additional resources.

10. Assist the client in determining a naturally occurring indicator which allows him to know that he is in the context where the change is desired. Establish a code name for the indicator.

11. Have the client experience the naturally occurring indicator and as he does so fire the anchor for the resource(s). This future paces the resource(s) to the desired context.

CHANGE HISTORY

Change history is a therapeutic technique which utilizes anchoring to assist clients in modifying their perceptions of past events in such a way as to change unpleasant and/or traumatic experiences into assets.[28] Some clients enter therapy with the preconceived idea that an event in their past is in some way limiting their choices in the present and future. For such clients, memories of unpleasant past events continue to intrude into day-to-day experiences. Many clients who enter therapy with a presenting problem that fits this format have a past primary time orientation. As in all therapeutic intervention, the first task of the therapist is to pace the client by meeting him at his model of the world. The change history paradigm focuses on altering the subjective experience of past events and therefore adequately paces a past-oriented person.

Since all experience is subjective, and memory is nothing more than a special category of subjective experience, it is possible to assist a client in altering his memories of past events so that such memories can be the source of resources instead of hinderance. In change history, the therapist facilitates by: guiding the client through fantasy, back to the experience which is acting as a liability; determining what resource(s) is needed to change the liability into an asset; gaining access to and anchoring the needed resource(s), using the client's entire repertoire of experience from which to choose; and, finally, making the anchored resource available in the context of the past event. Once this procedure is complete, the client has a different experience of the past event; one which offers additional choices and options.

Transcript

Pam is a 31-year old woman who has been married for the past ten years. Upon entering treatment, Pam was very clear about not loving her husband, however, due to having a painful affair five years ago she was unwilling to look at options in the areas of getting a divorce and possibly pursuing a more satisfying relationship. When Pam began treatment she was aware that the affair and the feelings attached to that experience were limiting her options in the present and future. The therapist used the change history paradigm as a way to alter her subjective experience of the memories of that past affair and, in doing so, was able to expand Pam's range of choices.

Therapist: What would you like to work on today?

Pam: I know I came into therapy two weeks ago in order to deal with my unhappy marriage and my fear of ending the relationship.

Therapist: What would you like to do about your marriage?

Pam: I would like to end my marriage and find someone who I could love, but each time I think about doing that the painful memories of my affair five years ago comes up.

Therapist: Would you like to be able to change your experience of that memory?

Pam: Yes.

Therapist: Take a moment, go back in time and re-experience a portion of that affair. More specifically, re-experience the portion of that affair that keeps reoccurring in your mind.

Pam: (Tears begin to form as skin becomes blotchy)

Therapist: (Reaches over and anchors that experience with a touch on Pam's right wrist)

What's going on?

Pam: I really loved him but he didn't want me.

Therapist: I know that is a painful memory for you but I'm wondering what resource would you need to make that memory okay?

(Pause)

Pam: I would need to change my focus from the painful outcome to the many wonderful experiences during the relationship.

Therapist: Would you need any other resources?

Pam: I would need to believe that the painful outcome of my affair was an isolated incident and that it is possible to have a loving relationship which endures.

Therapist: Take a moment and go back in time, and find an experience when you were able to focus on the positives of a relationship with another.

(Pause)

Pam: (Eyes closed as lip size swells, skin flushes and muscle tone becomes relaxed)

Therapist: (Reaches over and anchors that experience with a touch on Pam's right thumb)

(Pause)

Pam, have you ever had an experience of having a loving relationship that endured?

Pam: (Opens eyes) No, I never have.

Therapist: Do you know of any couple that have?

Pam: Yes, my friend, Cynthia.

Therapist: Can you imagine what it would be like to be Cynthia?

Pam: (Closes eyes and after a few moments muscle tone becomes very relaxed, breathing is slow and even)

Therapist: (Reaches over and anchors that experience by touching Pam's left wrist)

Now take a moment, go back in time to the experience of your affair.

(Fires anchor by touching right wrist)

Pam: (Eyes closed; skin becomes slightly blotchy and muscle tone is tense)

Therapist: As you go through that experience realize that you have new resources to go with you.

(Fires off resource anchors by holding right thumb and left wrist while continuing to hold down anchor on right wrist)

Pam:	(Eyes closed; muscle tone becomes relaxed, breathing is slow and even, skin is slightly flushed)

(Pause)

Therapist:	How was that experience for you?
Pam:	It was much better, but there is still something missing.
Therapist:	What additional resource do you need?

(Pause)

Pam:	I would need to believe that I am loveable.
Therapist:	Have you ever had that experience?
Pam:	Oh yeah, with my first boyfriend when I was sixteen. You know, back then I really felt loveable.
Therapist:	Good, take a moment and go back in time and re-experience feeling loveable.
Pam:	(Eyes open; throws back her head with laughter as she curls her feet under her, blushing slightly and giggles)
Therapist:	(Reaches over and touches Pam on the right index finger)

(Pause)

Therapist:	Now, take a moment, go back in time again to

	your memory of your affair (fires anchor by touching right wrist)
Pam:	(Closes eyes, skin becomes slightly flushed)
Therapist:	And as you go through that experience take these new resources with you.
	(Fires off resource anchors by holding down right thumb, left wrist, and right index finger while continuing to hold down anchor on right wrist)
Pam:	(Eyes closed, muscle tone becomes relaxed, breathing slow and even, as she smiles)
Therapist:	How is the experience now?
Pam:	Fine.
Therapist:	Take a moment and project yourself into the future and, as you do so, go through a couple of situations in which you meet new men and begin to explore new options in relationships.
Pam:	(Eyes closed; muscle tone is relaxed, breathing slow and even with a slight smile on her face)
Therapist:	(Notices minimal cues associated with resource states)
	(A few moments pass)
Therapist:	How was that for you?

Pam: I am beginning to believe that there were many special times in my past relationship and that I can open myself to new and exciting experiences in the future.

Algorithm for Change History

1. Identify the specific change desired.

2. Identify the experience from the past which the client believes is limiting present and future options.

3. Assist the client in re-experiencing the past event and establish an anchor for that experience.

4. Verify the anchor.

5. Assist the client in determining which resource is needed in order to change the subjective experience.

6. Assist the client in gaining access to the resource and establish an anchor for resource state.

7. Verify the anchor.

8. Assist the client in re-experiencing the past event with the newly acquired resource.

9. Collapse the anchors for the past experience and the resource state.

10. Verify that the outcome is a desirable one; if not, return to step 5 to gather additional resources.

11. Verify the change by future pacing the client.

CHANGE HISTORY WITH
TRANSDERIVATIONAL SEARCH

There are times when clients enter treatment with a sense that an event in their past is somehow limiting them in the present and future. These clients, however, are not conscious of the specific event(s), they are only aware of the feeling(s) involved. In such instances, the therapist can anchor the feeling and, using the feeling as a guide, assist the client in tracking back through time in order to reattach the feeling to the event in which it originally occurred. This tracking process is an application of transderivational search. Once the client is able to identify the original experience, the therapist can use the change history paradigm to assist the client in anchoring new resources into the old experience, thereby changing or reconstructing it to become a more positive experience.

Transcript

Jacqueline is a 41-year old female who is currently employed as an R.N. in a local hospital emergency room. Client entered therapy due to the fact that she had a problem coping with her job situation.

Therapist: What specific change would you like for yourself today?

Jacqueline: I would like to cope better with my job.

Therapist: Well, what is going on?

Jacqueline: I just feel very inadequate at work.

Therapist: Are you performing your duties appropriately?

Jacqueline: I know that I am doing a good job, getting all my work done and, in fact, I always get superior evaluations from my supervisor, but I feel so inadequate.

Therapist: Take a moment and get in touch with those feelings of inadequacy.

Jacqueline: (Eyes shift down, to the right; flick up, to the left; and then back down, to the right)

                Okay, I've got the feeling.

Therapist: (Notices the minimal cues; increased breathing rate, constricted lips and paleness. In addition, therapist notices K-V^r-K pattern)

Therapist: (Reaches over and touches Jacqueline on the index finger of her left hand to anchor the feeling)

Therapist: As you were experiencing those feelings of inadequacy were you aware of any images in your mind?

Jacqueline: No, just those feelings.

Therapist: Take a moment and get back in touch with the feelings (reaches over and touches client on her left index finger), and as you do, allow those feelings to float up into an image.

Jacqueline: (Eyes shift down, to the right and then up, to the left)

Therapist: What image are you seeing?

Jacqueline: I'm seeing my husband's last drunk.

Therapist: How do you feel when your husband drinks?

Jacqueline: (Eyes shift down and to the right)

                I feel inadequate. I can't seem to help him stay sober. (Eyes begin to tear)

Therapist: Stay with the experience. (Notices minimal cues; increased breathing rate, constricted lips and paleness. Therapist reaches over and anchors that experience on the client's left forefinger)

Therapist: Have there been other times in your life that you have felt inadequate?

Jacqueline: I have felt inadequate most of my life.

Therapist: Take a moment and again get in touch with those feelings (reaches over and touches client on her left index finger) and as you get in touch with those feelings allow them to take you back in time. As you go back through time, using those feelings as a guide, become aware of which experiences they are tied to.

                (A few moments pass)

Therapist: Let me know when you have identified any past experiences.

Jacqueline: (Breathing rapid and shallow, lips tighten and skin pales)

Jacqueline:	Okay, I have one.
Therapist:	(Reaches over and touches client on left ring finger in order to anchor experience) Where are you?
Jacqueline:	Back in my first marriage, he too was an alcoholic.
Therapist:	Continue to track back through time to an even earlier experience (fires off anchor by touching left index finger) (A few moments pass)
Jacqueline:	(Breathing becomes rapid and shallow, lips tighten and skin pales drastically)
Therapist:	(Reaches over and anchors experience by touching the client's left pinky finger) Where are you now?
Jacqueline:	I'm five years old, my daddy's drunk, he's hitting mom and I don't know what to do.
Therapist:	Come back to the here and now. (Pause) I'm wondering how these past experiences relate to your situation at work?
Jacqueline:	Many alcoholics come through the emergency room and the more I think about it; that's

when I feel inadequate.

Therapist:	What resources would you need in order to not feel inadequate in those past situations?
Jacqueline:	I would have to accept that alcoholism is a disease and that alcoholics are responsible for their recovery.
Therapist:	Have you ever had an experience of accepting that?
Jacqueline:	Sure, while in nursing school I had two semesters of substance abuse education.
Therapist:	Take a moment and go back to those classes and re-experience the knowledge of alcoholism as a disease and the role of the alcoholic in the recovery process.
Jacqueline:	(Eyes close; lips swell, breathing is even and skin flushes slightly)
Therapist:	(Reaches over and touches client on her right knee in order to anchor experience)

(Pause)

Can you think of any other resource that you need?

Jacqueline:	Well, I guess I need to realize that I am not a little girl and I can react differently to alcoholic situations.
Therapist:	Have you ever experienced that realization?

Jacqueline: Yes.

Therapist: Take a moment and re-experience that reali-
               zation now.

Jacqueline: (Eyes close, lips swell, breathing is even and
               skin flushes slightly)

Therapist: (Reaches over and touches client's right knee)

               Now, can you think of any additional resour-
               ces that you might need?

Jacqueline: The only other thing I can think of is confi-
               dence.

Therapist: Can you think of a time when you had confi-
               dence?

Jacqueline: (Leans forward) Of course.

Therapist: Take your time and re-experience that confi-
               dence.

Jacqueline: (Eyes close; lips swell, breathing is even and
               skin flushes slightly)

Therapist: (Reaches over and touches client on the right
               knee. Therapist has stacked all three resources
               on the same anchor)

                              (Pause)

               Okay, come back to the here and now.

Jacqueline: (Nods head)

Therapist: Jacqueline, what I am going to do now is have you go back to those past experiences in your life with these new resources in order for you to obtain a more desirable outcome.

Jacqueline: Okay.

Therapist: Now, taking those feelings of inadequacy (fires off anchor by touching left index finger), go to that experience of your husband drinking (fires off anchor by touching client's left forefinger); although this time these new resources will accompany you. (Fires off resource anchor by touching client's right knee. Therapist continues to touch left index finger, left forefinger and right knee simultaneously while client goes through this new experience.)

(Pause)

Therapist: (Notices minimal cues; body leaned forward slightly, skin color flushed, breathing rate even and lips swelled slightly)

(Pause)

Jacqueline: Okay.

Therapist: Now take those feelings (discontinues anchor for situation with current husband by no longer touching client's left forefinger) and go back to the situation with your first husband. (Fires off anchor by touching client's left ring finger. As the client goes through this experience the therapist continues to touch the anchors on client's left index finger, left ring finger and right knee simultaneously)

(Pause)

Therapist: (Notices minimal cues: skin color flushed, breathing rate even, lips swelled and body slightly leaned forward)

Jacqueline: Okay.

Therapist: Now take those feelings (discontinues anchor for situation with first husband by no longer touching client's left ring finger) and go even farther back in time to the situation in your childhood (fires off anchor for childhood experience by touching client's pinky finger. As the client goes through this experience the therapist continues to touch the anchors on the client's left index finger, left pinky finger and right knee simultaneously)

(Pause)

Therapist: (Notices minimal cues: skin color slightly flushed, breathing rate even, lips swelled and body slightly leaned forward)

Jacqueline: Okay.

Therapist: How was that for you?

Jacqueline: Fine, I was able to re-experience those memories in a very different way.

Therapist: Good, now I want you to project yourself into the future and imagine yourself at work and seeing an alcoholic patient being brought in through emergency.

Jacqueline: Okay. (Closes eyes)

Therapist: (Notices minimal cues; skin color slightly flushed, breathing rate even, lips swelled and body slightly leaned forward)

(Pause)

Therapist: How was that for you?

Jacqueline: Fine.

Alogrithm for Change History with Transderivational Search

1. Identify the unpleasant feeling.

2. Establish an anchor for the unpleasant feeling.

3. Hold the anchor constant while tracking back through the client's personal history for situations that have the same feeling.

4. Establish a separate anchor for each experience retrieved.

5. Assist the client in determining what resource(s) is needed in order to make a positive change in the past experiences.

6. Establish an anchor for the resource(s).

7. Collapse each past experience anchor with the resource(s) anchor.

8. Verify the change by future pacing.

ASSOCIATION

Association is a therapeutic technique which is best used in treating clients who have a future time orientation. This technique can be adapted to any of the three representational systems (V-A-K); however, it is primarily used when working with visual clients. Association is a subtle blend of representational systems, overlap, and anchoring.

The first step in the association process is that of assisting the client in making a visual image of himself as he would like to be, that is to say, with the desired change. The next step is to have the client step into the picture and, using overlap, guide him to the auditory and kinesthetic portions of the five tuple. The therapist then establishes an anchor for this newly acquired experience and by stimulus-stimulus conditioning, future paces that experience to the desired context. Association is an extremely simple, eloquent therapeutic intervention which assists the client in moving directly forward from the present state to the desired state.

Transcript

Client is a 25-year old man who entered therapy because he is having problems meeting women and more specifically asking women out on dates. Client shared that there were several women he knew as friends at work, church and in his apartment complex whom he would like to date, however, has been unable to get up the "nerve" to ask them out.

Therapist: What specific change would you like for yourself today?

Client: Well, I'd like to be able to ask a woman out on a date but when I go to do so I get nervous and freeze.

Therapist:	How would you like to feel in that situation?
Client:	Comfortable, confident and attractive. Sometimes I just don't feel attractive enough to be desirable.
Therapist:	Fine, make a visual image of yourself the way you would like to be in that situation with comfort, confidence and feelings of being attractive.
Client:	(Eyes defocus, pupils dialate, muscle tone in face flattens) (Pause) Okay, I've got the picture.
Therapist:	Good, now step into that picture and have the feelings of being there.
Client:	(Eyes refocus, muscle tone returns to face, slight flushing of the skin color, breathing even and slow, client adjusts body posture to an erect solid position) I can feel the confidence, comfort and being attractive.
Therapist:	Good, see the world through those eyes and hear the world through those ears and, if necessary, adjust your internal dialogue to one that is congruent with your current feelings.

(Pause)

Client:	Okay, I've got it.
Therapist:	(Reaches over and touches client on his right shoulder to anchor the experience)

(Pause)

Fine, now clear consciousness.

(Pause)

(Reaches over and touches client's right shoulder to test anchor, therapist notices minimal cues of slight flushing of skin color in the face, client assumes erect body posture and breathing rate becomes slow and even)

Client: That's strange, when you touch my shoulder I feel comfrotable, confident, and attractive again.

Therapist: That's right. Now, what's the first thing that you notice which lets you know that you're in a situation where you want these new resources?

Client: (Eyes shift up and to the right) Seeing an attractive woman (eyes shift down and to the left) and telling myself that I'd like to ask her for a date.

Therapist: (Notices the V-Ad sequence) Good, now make an image of an attractive woman and then tell yourself that you would like to ask her for a date.

Client: (Eyes shift up and to the right, then down and to the left)

Therapist: (Reaches over and touches client's right shoulder to fire anchor, just after client accesses the Ad step.

(Pause)

Now in your mind go through a situation in the future of seeing an attractive woman and asking her for a date.

Client: (Eyes shift up and to the right, then down and to the left, then down and to the right. Client's skin color is slightly flushed, breathing rate is slow and even and client adjusts body posture to a solid erect position)

(A moment passes)

Therapist: How did it turn out?

Client: Fine. I was able to ask her for a date, feeling confident, comfortable and attractive.

Algorithm for Association

1. Identify the desired change.

2. Assist the client in making a visual image of himself with the desired change (resource state).

3. Have the client step into the image.

4. Assist the client in experiencing the visual, auditory and kinesthetic portions of the resource state by using overlap of representational systems.

5. Establish an anchor for the resource state.

6. Test the anchor.

7. Future pace the resource state by attaching the anchor to a naturally occurring indicator of the desired context.

8. Test the work by having the client go through a situation in the future where the new resource state is wanted.

THREE PLACE DISASSOCIATION

There are situations in working with clients when a specific stimulus in the environment triggers such an intense kinesthetic response that it is impossible to use collapsing anchors directly in order to implement a more desirable outcome. Collapsing anchors has been the primary means of evolution in all the techniques previously mentioned in this chapter. In phobic situations, straight collapsing of anchors is ineffective because the kinesthetic response involved is so intense, overwhelming, and immobilizing that regardless of the number or the intensity of resources anchored, an integration will not occur. As previously mentioned, in order to integrate anchors, the experiences involved must be of approximately the same intensity. In the case of a phobia, it is impossible to gather resources that are as intense as the phobic response.

Three place or V-K disassociation is a process which integrates the techniques of visualization, anchoring, and progressive desensitization.[29] In three place disassociation, the therapist uses transderivational search to assist the client in tracking the phobic response back through time to the original experience which is the root of the phobia. Once the client has identified the root experience, he is instructed to view the past scene as a still picture, like that of a snapshot. By being in a disassociated position, seeing a picture of the younger self, any feelings involved will be meta feelings, that is, feelings about the experience and not the feelings of being there. From this disassociated position there are far more options available for collapsing anchors because what is being integrated is the visual and auditory portions of the past experience with the kinesthetic portion from the meta position. In a sense, the therapist is assisting the client in constructing a new five tuple. In most cases, in order to create a more satisfactory five tuple, the therapist integrates additional resources into the experience by anchoring those resources to the meta position. The final step in the three place disassociation process is having the client see and hear the entire scene from the past with the newly anchored resources.

Transcript

Client is a 42-year old woman who entered therapy with the presenting problem of having a phobia of elevators. Client was seen for one session, which lasted for approximately 65 minutes, and has since been able to ride elevators comfortably.

Therapist:	What do you want to work on during this session?
Client:	I have a phobia of elevators.
Therapist:	Fine, as you're sitting there in your chair take a moment and imagine yourself in an elevator.
Client:	Okay (Eyes close)
	(Pause)
	(Clutches chair, body becomes rigid, breathing is rapid and shallow as skin loses color.)

Therapist: (Reaches over and touches client on her left shoulder to anchor the experience)

               Okay, now clear consciousness.

Client: (Opens eyes, color returns to skin, body begins to relax and breathing becomes even and slow)

Therapist: Fine, now before we go any further I would like to establish an anchor or a marker with you for comfort so that as we work on this phobia we can do so with you feeling comfortable.

Client: (Nods)

Therapist: (Reaches over and takes client's left hand in his) I'm going to hold your hand and as I do so I want you to squeeze my hand each time you access the experiences I'm going to describe.

Client: (Nods)

Therapist: I'd like you to remember an experience of being very relaxed and comfortable.

Client: Okay. (Eyes close)

               (Pause)

               (Breathing becomes slow and deep, skin flushes and body relaxes, client squeezes therapist's hand)

Therapist: (Notices the minimal cues and feels the client squeezing his hand. The therapist establishes an anchor for the experience by squeezing the client's hand)

(Pause)

Client: (Eyes open)

Therapist: Good, now can you remember a time when you felt confident?

Client: Sure.

Therapist: Go back and feel those feelings of confidence.

Client: (Eyes close)

(Pause)

(Lips swell, skin flushes and body posture becomes erect, client squeezes therapist's hand)

Therapist: (Notices the minimal cues and feels the client squeezing his hand. The therapist establishes an anchor for the confidence by squeezing the client's hand)

(Pause)

Client: (Eyes open)

Therapist: Has there ever been a time in your life when you thought that you couldn't do something but surprised and delighted yourself by doing it magnificently? (This resource is an access

	to the unconscious mind or unconscious resources)
Client:	Sure.
Therapist:	Okay, go back to that experience and re-experience it.
Client:	(Eyes close, lips swell slightly, breathing rate becomes deep and even, client squeezes therapist's hand)
Therapist:	(Notices the minimal cues, feels the client squeezing his hand. The therapist establishes an anchor by squeezing the client's hand)

(Pause)

Client:	(Eyes open)
Therapist:	Good, now take these feelings (reaches over and touches client on her left shoulder firing the anchor for the phobic experience) and go back through time with them (client closes eyes), going as far back as possible, knowing that I'm here with you. (Squeezes left hand slightly) As you go back, find an experience to which the feeling is attached. And then see yourself in that scene as if you are looking at a snapshot and know that you can do so with comfort and confidence because you are seeing that younger you while sitting here with me.

(Pause)

Client: I have a scene.

Therapist: What's going on?

Client: I can see myself at age three, or maybe four, being stuck in an elevator at a local department store and I'm alone.

Therapist: Okay, good. Hold that scene as a still picture and as you do so, imagine yourself floating up out of your body so that you can see yourself sitting comfortably with me, watching the picture of the younger you.

                              (Pause)

Client: Okay.

Therapist: Now, in a moment I'm going to have you let the scene from the past play as if you are watching a movie. You will see and hear the experiences from your past but you will keep the feelings of comfort, confidence and delight (squeezes client's left hand) from the present. Do you understand?

Client: Yes.

Therapist: If at any time you begin to feel any discomfort just squeeze my hand.

Client: Okay.

Therapist: Let the scene roll and see yourself seeing yourself and, as you do so, you can learn something special.

Client: (Nods)

                 (Slight pause)

                 (Breathing rate becomes deep and even, lips
                 swell slightly, skin flushes, and body relaxes)

                 (Pause)

                 (Body tenses slightly, client squeezes thera-
                 pist's hand gently)

Therapist: (Notices slight tensing of client's body as she
                 squeezes his hand. Therapist fires resource
                 anchor by squeezing client's hand)

Client: (Body relaxes)

                 (Pause)

                 Okay, I've gone through the entire scene and
                 I've learned something by seeing it from this
                 perspective.

Therapist: Fine, now float back down into your body.

Client: Okay.

Therapist: Is there something that you could say to the
                 younger self to reassure her that you grew up
                 to be a competent, successful and happy
                 adult?

Client: Yes.

Therapist: Then do so.

(Pause)

Client: Okay.

Therapist: Now reach out and pick up the younger you
                and pull her into your chest. You know that
                she is a part of you and that you are who you
                are today partly because of her experiences.

Client: (Reaches out with her arms and pulls the
                imagined younger part into her chest)

                (Pause)

                (Muscle tone in the face flattens out starting
                at the sides of the face and moving toward the
                front, a slight flushing of the neck occurs)

Therapist: How was that for you?

Client: Good.

Therapist: Now, imagine yourself in an elevator.

Client: Okay. (Eyes close) (Pause)

                (Skin flushes slightly, breathing rate becomes
                deep and even, lips swell slightly, body relaxes)

                (Pause)

Therapist: How did that turn out?

Client: (Nods) Good, I felt comfortable.

Therapist then instructed the client to go for a ride in the elevator which was located in the building next door. The client returned after about 15 minutes and reported a comfortable ride.

Algorithm for Three Place Disassociation

1. Elicit and establish an anchor for the traumatic experience.

2. Elicit and establish an anchor for resource(s).

3. While holding anchor for resource(s), fire the anchor for the traumatic experience and, using transderivational search, track back to the original experience.

4. Assist the client in experiencing only the visual and auditory portions of the original experience as a snapshot.

5. While continuing to hold the resource anchor, assist the client in disassociating by having him float up and watch himself seeing the younger him.

6. While client is disassociated, with the resource(s) anchor held, have him see and hear the original scene as a moving picture.

7. Assist the client in floating back to the self and then have the client reassure the younger self.

8. Have the client integrate the younger self.

PART IV

Experience is not what happens to you, it is what you do with what happens to you.

Aldous Huxley

23

REFRAMING

Experience in and of itself is neither positive nor negative; it is the judgment made about the experience which gives it meaning. Primary experience is the information gathered through the senses which is then stored in memory; whether these experiences add to our repertoire of resources or burden us as liabilities is the result of thoughts and feelings about or meta to the experience. Reframing is a technique which allows the client to change the meta feelings and thoughts which are connected to the experience and in that way change experiences once judged negative into positive.

To reframe, then, means to change the conceptual and/or emotional setting or viewpoint in relation to which a situation is experienced and to place it in another frame which fits the "facts" of the same concrete situation equally well or even better, and thereby changes its entire meaning.[30]

Reframing stands on the principle that all behavior, no matter how maladaptive it may seem, is adaptive given the context in which it was originally learned.[31] Furthermore, behind all behavior there exists a positive intent. Often the seemingly maladaptive behavior is the result of decisions made on an unconscious level, which have become nominalized in time and as such are no longer appropriate given the client's current resources and state of being.

Content Reframe

Content reframing is a linguistic pattern which allows the therapist to quickly redefine the meaning of certain experiences in the client's life. This redefinition allows the client to change his perspective of the experience so that it may become a resource.

Example:

Client: My husband is really driving me crazy, he is always hanging around, wanting to talk. You know, being underfoot.

Therapist: Isn't it nice to know that he cares so much about you that he wants to be near you and share his experiences with you.

Example:

Client: My ex-wife was a real terror. All she did was complain, boss me around and make my life miserable. I don't ever want to get involved with another woman.

Therapist: Aren't you glad to know that you really know what you don't want in a relationship so that now you can go out and get what you do want.

Example:

Client: After eight months of sobriety, I got drunk Saturday night. I thought I could have just one.

Therapist: It must be good to know that you are really powerless over alcohol and you never need to drink again.

SIX STEP REFRAMING MODEL

The six step reframing model is a formal procedure which separates behavior from intent and works to assist the client in satisfying the secondary gains that are involved in the behavior/symptom.[32] By satisfying the secondary gains the therapist can implement change in such a way as not to interfere with the client's personal ecology.

Transcript

Client is a 24 year old woman who entered treatment with a presenting problem of migraine headaches. The client stated that her migraine headaches are preceded by the typical aura stage and the headaches are often accompanied by nausea.

Therapist: What do you want to work on?

Client: You know that I have migraine headaches. I've been on medication and my doctor thought that since I'm seeing a therapist, you might be able to help.

Therapist: Okay. What I want you to do is go inside and make contact with the part of you responsible for the migraines.

(Pause)

Client: (Closes eyes)

(Pause)

(Eyes remain closed) Okay.

Therapist: Ask that part if it has a positive intention.

(Pause)

Client: (Eyes remain closed) I'm not getting an answer.

Therapist: Did you experience anything?

Client: (Eyes open) I (Eyes shift down and to the right, K^1) had the feelings which usually accompany the aura stage of my migraines.

Therapist: Have those feelings reoccur if that part of you has a positive intention.

Client: (Closes eyes, flushes slightly) I had the feelings again.

Therapist: Go inside and ask the part responsible for the migraines if it's willing to let you know what the positive intention is and, if so, to do so.

(Pause)

Client: (Eyes open) I (eyes up and to the left, V^r) know what the intention is. You see I work very hard at my job as a real estate agent. Many times I work seven days a week, twelve hours a day until I am exhausted. When I get a migraine about every six to seven weeks I end up in bed for at least two days. The migraines make me rest.

Therapist: Good. Go inside and contact your creative part and ask her to come up with three new ways to satisfy that positive intention which does not involve harming you in any way. Once your creative part has generated these three new ways let me know.

Client: Alright. (Closes eyes)

               (A few minutes pass)

               (Eyes open) I've got the three new ways.

Therapist: Go inside and ask the part responsible for the migraines to look at these three new ways and if it agrees that they satisfy the positive intention to signal you with the aura stage feelings.

Client: (Closes eyes)

               (Pause)

               (Slight flushing) I had the feelings.

Therapist:	Now, go inside and ask the part of you responsible for the migraines, if for the next ten weeks, it would implement these three new creative options in the place of the old symptoms. If so, to have those aura stage feelings occur.
Client:	(Closes eyes, slight flushing begins to occur)
	(Pause)
	(Eyes open) I had those feelings.
Therapist:	Thank those parts for cooperating with you, however, ask them now to be silent and ask if any other part objects to this new arrangement.
Client:	(Eyes close)
	(Pause)
	(Eyes open) There are no objections.
Therapist:	Now, we have made an arrangement that will cover the next ten weeks and if this new arrangement works for you it can continue indefinitely. However, if any new arrangements need to be made this can occur in the naturally integrating time known as dreaming.
Client:	(Nods head) Okay.

Algorithm for Six Step Reframing Model

1. Identify the behavior and contact the part that generates the behavior.

2. Separate the intention from the behavior.

3. Verify that the intention is positive.

4. Have the creative part generate three ways to satisfy the intention.

5. Verify that the part responsible for the behavior agrees that the three new ways will satisfy the intention and determine if it's willing to use these three new ways instead of the old behavior. (A time limit may be necessary) Have the part responsible for the behavior implement these three new ways in the place of the old behavior.

6. Verify that all parts agree to this new arrangment. If there are any parts which object to this arrangement, backtrack to step 2. If there are no objections, have client thank all parts for their cooperation.

CONTEXTUAL REFRAMING

Contextual reframing is very similar to the six step model, except that it makes the assumption that all behaviors are useful in some contexts.[33] The process of contextual reframing attaches the behavior to the context(s) where it is appropriate and eliminates the behavior from all other contexts.

Transcript

Client is a 34 year old male with the presenting problem of anxiety which is related to compulsivity.

Therapist: What specific change would you like for yourself today?

Client: I'm always feeling anxious, worrying about every detail. I can't seem to relax. In fact, when I'm trying to have fun with friends or my family I can't relax and enjoy myself, I just feel nervous. When I feel nervous and worry constantly, I always feel tired, burned out and in fact feeling like this I don't even get my work done.

Therapist: Do you feel that this anxiety serves any positive function in your life?

(Pause)

Client: Sure, it does at times motivate me to get work done, however, now it seems out of control.

Therapist: Okay. Go inside and make contact with the part of you responsible for the axiety.

(Pause)

Client: Okay.

Therapist: Did you make contact?

Client: Yes.

Therapist: How do you know you made contact?

Client: I felt the anxiety.

Therapist: Good, we can use the anxiety as a means of communication with that part of you. Now, go inside and ask that part if it has a positive intent and if so to communicate with you by allowing those feelings to occur again.

(Pause)

Client: I had the feelings again.

Therapist: Since that part of you has a positive intent, ask that part along with the help of your creative part to sort through the possible contexts or situations where the anxiety truly serves the positive intent and functions in a useful way. Once those parts have secured the contexts where the anxiety does serve a positive function have it signal you with the feelings.

Client: Okay.

(Pause)

I had the feelings.

Therapist: Go inside and ask the part of you responsible for anxiety if it would be in charge of allowing the anxiety to occur only in the contexts where it serves the positive function for the next two months and if it agrees to this to signal you.

(Pause)

Client: I got the feelings.

Therapist: Now thank those parts for cooperating with you, however, ask them now to be silent and ask if any parts object to this new arrangement.

(Pause)

Client: There are no objections.

Therapist: Good, now that we have done this piece of
                 work, these arrangements will cover the next
                 two months and may continue indefinitely,
                 however, if at any point you need to make
                 any new negotiations they can occur during
                 the dream process.

Algorithm for Contextual Reframing

1. Identify the behavior/symptom and contact the part that
    generates the behavior.

2. Separate the intention from the behavior.

3. Verify that the intention is positive.

4. Have the part responsible for the behavior together with
    the creative part determine in which context(s) the be-
    havior serves the positive intention.

5. Have the part responsible for the behavior be responsible
    to implement the behavior only in those context(s).

6. Verify that all parts agree to this new arrangement. (Eco-
    logical check)

ANCHORING WITH REFRAMING

Anchoring and reframing are two techniques that can
easily be combined. When used together, anchoring enables
the therapist to assist the client in integrating disassociated

states of consciousness and/or restructuring subjective experiences. Once accomplished, the six step reframing model or the contextual reframing model is used to satisfy the secondary gains.

Transcript

Client is a 26 year old woman who entered treatment to quit smoking cigarettes. Client began smoking at age 16 and currently smokes 1½ to 2 packs per day.

Therapist: What brings you here today?

Client: I want to quit smoking.

Therapist: How long have you smoked?

Client: Ten years.

Therapist: How much do you smoke?

Client: One and one-half to two packs per day.

Therapist: Have you ever tried to quit before?

Client: Yes, but I can't seem to do it.

Therapist: Okay, I'm going to ask you to have a couple of experiences and as you access these experiences I'm going to touch you on the knees so as to mark the experiences for future reference.

Client: Fine.

Therapist: Has there ever been a time when you have really enjoyed a cigarette?

Client: Oh yes, right after meals.

Therapist: Good, go back to one of those times and re-experience that enjoyment.

(Pause)

Therapist: (Notices minimal cues, reaches over and touches client on left knee to anchor the experience)

(Pause)

Okay, now clear consciousness.

(Pause)

Client: Okay.

Therapist: Have you ever had the experience of waking up in the morning, coughing, with that burnt taste in your mouth, your hair smelling of smoke and feeling disgusted with your filthy habit?

Client: Yes.

Therapist: Take a moment and get in touch with that experience.

(Pause)

Therapist: (Notices minimal cues, reaches over and

touches client on right knee to anchor the experience)

(Pause)

Now clear consciousness.

(Pause)

Client: Okay.

Therapist: (Tests anchors and verifies that they are firmly installed)

Now (reaches over and touches both of client's knees simultaneously) as you have this new experience you may find that additional choices and options become available to you.

(Pause)

(Notices that an integration has occurred)

Now, go inside and contact the part of you responsible for the smoking behavior.

(Pause)

Client: Okay, I made contact.

Therapist: How do you know that you made contact?

Client: I saw an image of my cigarette pack.

Therapist: Go inside and ask the part of you responsible for smoking if she has a positive intention and

if she does, have her signal you by again show-
ing you the image of the cigarette pack.

(Pause)

Client: Okay, I saw the image.

Therapist: Now, ask that part if she is willing to let you
know in consciousness what the positive in-
tention is and if so to please do so; if she is
not willing to let you know then to signal you
with the image.

(Pause)

Client: I saw the image.

Therapist: Now go inside and ask your creative part to
come up with three new ways to satisfy the
intention and once she has the three ways to
signal you with the image of the cigarette
pack.

(Pause)

Client: I saw the image.

Therapist: Good, now ask the part of you responsible for
the smoking to review these three new op-
tions and if she agrees that these options
satisfy the positive intention to signal you
with the image.

(Pause)

Client: Okay, I got the image.

Therapist:	Now again go inside and this time ask the part responsible for smoking if she would be willing to implement these three new options in the place of the old smoking behavior for the next two months. If she is willing to do so to signal you with the image.

(Pause)

Client:	I saw the image.

Therapist:	Thank those parts for cooperating with you and ask them now to be silent while you go inside and ask if there are any objections to this new arrangement.

(Pause)

Client:	There are no objections.

Therapist:	During this session we have made a new arrangement which will last for the next two months and if this new arrangement works for you it can continue indefinitely; however, if any additional arrangements need to be made, this can occur using this same format, during the naturally integrative state of sleep and dreaming.

STRATEGY FOR UPTIME

Uptime is a state of consciousness in which all parameters of the 5 tuple are focused externally (V^e, A^e, K^e, O^e, G^e). While in uptime, the therapist has no internal experiences and is therefore able to systematically notice and utilize the client's responses. In this state of consciousness, the therapist becomes intimately involved in a biofeedback loop with the environment.

Procedure for Uptime

1. Establish a self anchor for external experience which includes all the parameters of the 5 tuple (V^e, A^e, K^e, O^e, G^e).

2. Establish a self anchor for internal experience which includes all the parameters of the 5 tuple (V^i, A^i, K^i, O^i, G^i).

3. Test each anchor to verify that they are firmly installed.

4. Use the six step reframing model to satisfy any objections to uptime.

5. Fire the anchor for external experience each time uptime is desired.

24

METAPHOR

Down through the ages, stories have been used for the purpose of entertainment, enchantment and teaching. In the cultural history of most people, there lies a vast storehouse of learnings known as folklore. These tales have no specifically known origins and are passed down by word of mouth from generation to generation. As in any art form, many of these stories have stood the test of time and offer learnings as relevant today as when they were first told. One culture, that is particularly rich in the use of metaphor as a teaching strategy, is the American Indian.

If you and I were sitting in a circle of people on the prairie, and if I were then to place a painted drum or an eagle feather in the middle of this circle, each of us would perceive these objects differently. Our vision of them would vary according to our individual positions in the circle, each of which would be unique.

Our personal perceptions of these objects would also depend upon much more than just the different positions from which we looked upon them. For example, one or more of us might suffer from color blindness, or from weak eyesight. Either of these two physical differences would influence our perceptions of the objects.

There are levels upon levels of perspectives we must consider when we try to understand our individual perceptions of things, or when we try to relate our own perceptions to those of our brothers and sisters. Every single one of our previous experiences in life will affect in some way the mental perspective from which we see the world around us.

Because of this, a particular object or event may appear fearful to you at the same time that it gives pleasure to me, or appears completely uninteresting to a third person. All things that we perceive stimulate our individual imaginations in different ways, which in turn causes us to create our own unique interpretations of them. Love, hate, fear, confusion, happiness, envy, and all the other emotions we feel, act upon us to paint our perceptions of things in different colors.

If the thing I were to place within our circle should be an abstraction, such as an idea, a feeling, or a philosophy, our perceptions of it would then be even more complicated than if the object had been a tangible thing. And further, the number of different perceptions of it would become greater and greater as more and more people were added to our circle. The perception of any object, either tangible or abstract, is ultimately made a thousand times more complicated whenever it is viewed within the circle of *an entire people as a whole*. The understanding of this truth is the first lesson of the Medicine Wheel, and it is a vital part of Sun Dance Teaching.

This brings us back again to the Medicines. Each

of us has as his personal Medicine a particular animal reflection. The characteristics of this reflection are determined by the nature of the animal itself, and also by the location of our individual Beginning Place on the Medicine Wheel. These two things, our Medicine Animal and our Beginning Place on the Medicine Wheel, together are the Beginning Gift to each of us from *Miaheyyun.*

For example, there are Eagle People, Elk People, Bear People, Wolf People, Pheasant People, Otter People, Buffalo People, Mice People, Rock People, Cloud People, and as many other kinds of People as there are kinds of living beings on this earth. And within each of these different kinds of People, there are other differences of the Four Great Directions. Thus an Elk Person might be born a White Elk of the North, a Green Elk of the South, a Black Elk of the West, or a Yellow Elk of the East, depending upon the Direction of their Beginning Gift.

It would be impossible for me to tell you here of all the different Medicines, but I will speak to you of one of them, the Mouse. Mice live all their lives next to the ground, building their nests and gathering their food among the roots of the tall grass and bushes of the prairie. Because of this, Mice never see things at a distance. Everything they can see is right in front of them, where they can sniff at it with their noses and Touch it with their whiskers. Their lives are spent in Touching things in this way, and in gathering seeds and berries to eat.

But since it is really people that we are talking about, the Medicines must be understood within the ways of the people. A Mouse Person would be one who saw everything close up, and whose vision would be limited to the immediate world around him. He would be a gatherer of things. He might gather facts, information, material objects, or even ideas. But because he could not see far enough to connect his world with that of the great prairie of the world around him, he would never be able to use or understand all that he was and gathered.

If a Mouse Person were to be born into the North, his Beginning Gift would be the Gift of the Mind. His Name might be White Mouse. He would be a wise Mouse Person, but he would not yet be Whole. To become Whole, he would first have to seek the South, the place of the Heart, and find the Marriage of this Gift with his Beginning Gift. Then he would have to visit and have Intercourse with the things of the East, Illumination, and travel to the Looks-Within place of the West. He would be able to Grow and become a Full Person only by doing all of these things, which would give him an understanding of his own Nature.

In this way he would become able to make his decisions within the Balance of the Four Directions. A person with the Beginning Gift of the Mind must always try to include his Heart in his decisions. When he does this, he begins to turn upon the Medicine Wheel. A man can live out his entire life without ever finding more than what was already within him as his Beginning Gift, but if he wishes to Grow he must become a Seeker and Seek for himself the other Ways.

When you have done this for yourself, and when you have reached a full Understanding of the different Medicines of men, you will never feel surprised or threatened by the actions or decisions of your Brothers and Sisters. This Understanding is held within the meaning of the Shields carried by the People, which were Mirrors of their Medicines.[34]

The use of metaphors is not isolated to the world of philosophers and shaman, in recent years metaphors have become a widely accepted therapeutic tool. Examples of the creative use of metaphors are best illustrated in the work of the late Milton H. Erickson, M.D. Erickson would often make therapeutic interventions, not directly by addressing the problem in conventional ways, but instead by the use of analogy or anecdote. One of the prime assets in using metaphors in the psychotherapeutic context, is that metaphors tend to work on an unconscious level and therefore by-pass resistance from the conscious mind. Erickson believed that significant changes occurred at the unconscious level and that metaphors allowed him to work more directly with the unconscious mind.

There seems to be a correlation between what Erickson called the unconscious and what neuro-psychologists refer to as non-dominant hemisphere (right hemisphere). The non-dominant hemisphere carries out integrative and artistic type processing. It seems that metaphors tap into and utilize right hemisphere functioning which helps unleash a client's own creativity.

A couple came in to see Dr. Erickson for conjoint therapy, with a presenting problem of sexual discord. The problem arose from the husband's desire to immediately have intercourse while the wife was engulfed in wanting to spend more time in foreplay. After hearing the presenting problem, Dr. Erickson changed the topic and went on to other subjects. Near the end of the session Erickson gave the couple the task of planning and cooking a meal together, with the wife preparing the entree and the husband the appetizers. After preparing the meal the couple were to sit down and enjoy the meal together.[35]

Language is not experience but instead, is about experience. Language in and of itself is a metaphor, a representation of experience. Words become symbols for items in sensory experience. When language is employed, all theory no matter how scientific in nature, becomes a metaphor, a symbolic representation. There is a continuum in the construction of metaphors which specifically deals with the amount of distance between language and experience. This continuum is that of a shallow metaphor versus a deep metaphor. The difference between these two types of metaphor is the degree of abstraction involved in the symbolism. To illustrate this point, many clinicians choose to deliver metaphors using other clients as the general topic. Within this design, there are a number of similarities between the client and the topic of the metaphor, such as: both are clients, both are people, and both want change. Using a semantic space (other clients) is an excellent example of a shallow metaphor. Should these same clinicians, however, use the general topic fairy tale, the level of abstraction would be greater and therefore a deep metaphor.

There are certain outcomes which are natural by-products of metaphor depth and, in choosing the depth of a metaphor several factors come into existence. A shallow metaphor is more likely to be interpreted and resisted by the conscious mind, whereas, a deep metaphor operates on an unconscious level. When working more directly with the unconscious, the therapist by-passes conscious resistance. Another factor to take into consideration is what topic or semantic space the therapist feels comfortable presenting to his clients. For some clinicians, it would be difficult to tell stories, such as: Fairy tales, animal stories, or science fiction, however, for other therapists, it would be perfectly acceptable to utilize the deeper semantic space.

Metaphor can be used as an effective tool in the therapeutic process for a number of reasons. First, metaphors are a very non-manipulative technique. In the use of metaphors, the therapist does not offer an interpretation, which, therefore, allows the client to derive his own meaning from and assign his own values to the story. Second, in the process of understanding the metaphor, the client must adopt an internal orientation, that is, go inside of himself and use his own life experiences in order to make sense out of the story. Many therapeutic processes include introspection as a primary tool. This process allows the client to begin to rely on himself and his own resources. Third, the metaphor is usually analyzed both consciously and unconsciously, however, its prime value as a therapeutic intervention is that of assisting the client in tapping into his own unconscious resources. The unconscious is a vast storehouse of experiences and learning which can be used as resources in order to make desired change.

Case Study

Client came into the session and stated that he had mixed feelings about returning to school. The client stated that he would really like to learn more and to improve himself, however, wasn't sure that he was willing to make a firm commitment to do the work necessary. The client stated that he felt torn and wanted to come to a decision.

The following metaphor was constructed and delivered to the client in order to help facilitate the process of deciding.

The King and His Kingdom

Once upon a time, there was a king who lived in a magical kingdom far away. One day it came to the king's attention that there was trouble in the northern province. The king knew that this trouble needed to be dealt with in order to restore a sense of peace, however, he was not sure how to do it. The king being disturbed by this trouble, thought about it all evening and when he went to bed he fell into a deep sleep. While in the deep sleep he had a dream in which he dreamed that he had a meeting of the officers of the kingdom. At this meeting there was present the minister of the interior, the minister of the exterior, the minister of health, education and welfare and the minister of natural resources. During the process of the meeting the cabinet officers were able to settle their business in such a way that each was satisfied. When the king awoke from his sleep he was joyous because he had learned a new way to solve the problem. The king went out and applied his new found talent to managing his kingdom.

WELL-FORMEDNESS

In order to ensure the effectiveness of a metaphor, there are a number of well-formedness conditions involved in the design. The well-formedness conditions for metaphor design are: 1) Isomorphism, 2) Semantic Space, 3) Goal Achievement, 4) Access to Resources, and 5) Future Pace.[36]

Isomorphism

The first well-formedness condition is that of isomorphism. The term isomorphis, is a concept borrowed from mathematics which means one-to-one mapping or a one-to-one relationship. In designing a metaphor it is important that there is a symbol in the metaphor which is equivalent to each character and event in the client's presenting problem. The most efficient way to maintain a one-to-one relationship is to decipher all nouns and process words (verbs, adverbs, and adjectives) in the presenting problem and assign a corresponding item in the metaphor. This step also establishes a pace with the client on an unconscious level.

Example from The King and His Kingdom:

Nouns

Case Study		Metaphor
Client	–	King
Client's Life	–	Kingdom
Client's Thinking	–	Northern Province

Processes

Case Study		Metaphor
Mixed Feelings	–	Dealing with Trouble
about School	–	in the Kingdom

As you will see later in this section, the isomorphic relationship will continue as the therapist begins to lead the client toward the goal and assists him in gaining access to the necessary resources for goal achievement.

Another pattern which is closely related to isomorphism is that of homomorphism. Homomorphism is a many-to-one relationship. When designing a metaphor employing a homomorphic relationship, one symbol stands for several similar items in the presenting problem. An illustration of this might be having one rose bush represent a client's family, even though the family has eight members.

Semantic Space

Semantic space, the second well-formedness condition, is the general content area which is to be used in the metaphor. Some examples of semantic space are: animal stories, science fiction stories, fairy tales, an incident from childhood, a former client, a friend, and children. The possibilities for semantic space are infinite for the creative therapist. When choosing the semantic space one can easily pace the client by utilizing the client's age, interests and talents. For example: telling a child a fairy tale; telling a florist a story about gardening; and telling an engineer a story about science. One way of choosing a semantic space which paces the client, but does not intrude into consciousness, is by changing the time reference. For example, telling a professional football player a story about the gladiators of ancient Rome.

Goal Achievement

As in all therapeutic techniques, goal achievement is an important issue. Many clients come to therapy with a specific goal or change in mind. The therapist must understand the goal and construct the metaphor in such a way as to be effective in assisting the client in the goal achievement process. The first portion of the metaphor should pace or join the client at his model of the world and as the metaphor develops it should lead the client toward goal achievement.

Access to Resources

Closely related to the previous well-formedness conditions is that of access to resources. This condition requires that within the metaphor, provisions are made for the client to gain access to the resources necessary in order to achieve the desired goal. In some cases, these resources might be as specific as relaxation, self confidence or assertiveness, however, they may also be more general, such as, a way to make decisions or to gain problem solving skills. It is invariably useful to incorporate an access to the unconscious in the resource section of the metaphor, which is often accomplished by having a *dream* occur within the story. The dream state is generally considered an archetype for unconscious processing. The metaphor is often designed to teach a client to rely upon his own resources, such as, intuition, tacit knowledge, integrating internal parts, and using past learning. In addition to gaining access to internal resources, a metaphor can easily assist a client in utilizing external resources, such as other people, books, school and seminars.

Future Pace

In order to be sure that the changes and resources are made available in the desired context, a future pacing step becomes the fifth and last well-formedness condition. Future pacing links the unconscious learnings and resources made available through metaphor to normal states of consciousness and, more specifically, to the presenting problem.

The King and His Kindom (Outlined)

When first learning to build metaphors, outlines of the design are useful in ensuring well-formedness. In the metaphor earlier presented, entitled The King and His Kingdom, it is easy to check and note that the well-formedness conditions are satisfied.

		Nouns		
		Case Study		Metaphor
P		Client	—	King
A		Client's Life	—	Kingdom
		Client's Thinking	—	Northern Province
C		Processes		
		Case Study		Metaphor
E		Mixed Feelings about School		Dealing with Trouble in the Kingdom

	Resources	
	Case Study	Metaphor
	Access to Unconscious Mind	— Dream
	Intuition	— Minister of Natural Resources
	Client's Internal Parts	— Minister of the Interior
	Outside Resources	— Minister of the Exterior
	Personal Integrity, Well Being and Education	— Minister of Health, Education and Welfare

	Goal	
	Case Study	Metaphor
	Make Decision	— Restore a Sense of Peace to the Kingdom

	Future Pace	
	Case Study	Metaphor
	Apply Decision Making Skills to the Problem of School	— Went Out and Applied His New Found Talent Managing the Kingdom

(left margin, vertically: L E A D)

Algorithm for Creating Metaphors

1. Elicit the case history.

2. Isolate the presenting problem.

3. Define the goal.

4. List the nouns.

5. List the process words (verbs, adverbs, adjectives).

6. Select the semantic space.

7. Create a noun for each noun in the presenting problem.

8. Create a process word for each process in the presenting problem.

9. Select the resources needed to achieve the desired goal.

10. Transfer these resources into metaphoric language consistent with the semantic space selected.

11. Establish the future pacing step and translate it into metaphoric space.

LANGUAGE PATTERNS

There are a number of language patterns which greatly enhance the therapist's effectiveness in utilizing metaphor. These patterns were introduced by Richard Bandler and John Grinder in "Patterns of the Hypnotic Techniques of Milton Erickson, M.D. Volume I." Although these patterns were first studied in the realm of hypnosis they are equally applicable in the use of therapeutic metaphors. The general term used for these linguistic patterns is the Milton Model. The Milton

Model allows the therapist to speak in a way that sounds very specific although upon a closer examination is actually very vague. When utilizing non-specific language, the only way a client can make sense out of the language, is by assigning his own meaning to the words. This is a particularly useful set of patterns which facilitates the client to adapt an internal orientation in order to find experiences that define the vague terms used. This technique also supports the idea of non-manipulation because it is the client's own experiences being assigned to the language patterns. These patterns are often referred to as "process" language because they do not specify content distinction, only process.

We, as human beings, make sense out of language by searching our own personal histories for experiences which are associated with or define the words. For example, when you read the word "comfort," the way that you determine the meaning of this word is by either remembering or imagining the experience of comfort and to some degree re-experiencing it. The process of associating a word to an internal representation which gives meaning to the word, as previously mentioned, is transderivational search. Although the process of transderivational search is a mechanism by which all language is understood, there are certain language patterns which are very non-specific and therefore, allow more variety in individually assigned meaning.

Lack of Referential Index

Lack of referential index is a linguistic pattern in which a category of objects/events is mentioned, however, reference is not made to a specific object/event in sensory experience. This pattern is an example of generalization because instead of representing a specific experience, it represents an entire category of experiences. In addition, lack of referential index is an example of deletion since the specific object/event to which it refers is deleted from the linguistic pattern.

Example:

> People can make changes.
> He was able to learn something special.
> Thomas learned something from it.
> . . . And the dream was important to her.

In the previous examples the underlined words have a lack of referential index. When this pattern is used, the person hearing the metaphor will usually interpret the sentence in such a way as to apply the sentence to himself, and in a way that is consistent with his own needs.

Lack of Referential Index with Suggested Noun Substitution

One way to more specifically indicate which noun you want substituted for the word which lacks referential index is to mention it in the sentence, however, out of the noun position.

Example:

> People, Mary, can change.
> People can, Mary, change.
> People can change, Mary.

This same pattern can be used in delivering a metaphor to ensure that the client relates himself to the desired character in the story.

Example:

> The prince, Joe, was puzzled.
> The prince was, Joe, puzzled.
> The prince was puzzled, Joe.

Unspecified Verbs

Unspecified verbs are verbs which do not indicate a full description of the action taking place. When utilizing metaphors, the deletion of material concerning the unspecified verb allows the client to fill in for himself a fuller description of the process being described. This fuller description will be one that is most congruent for the client based on his own personal resources.

Example:

And the prince <u>understood</u> what was being offered to him.

Joan <u>knew</u> something was different.

David will be able to <u>learn</u> about himself.

Nominalization

Nominalization is a process whereby a (verb) is changed into an object (noun). Once this change has occurred, much information about the process is deleted. Employing nominalizations, in the context of metaphor, allows the client to assign his own process to replace the information deleted. The process information which the client assigns to the nominalization will come from his own model of the world and, therefore, presupposes his reliance on personal resources.

Verbs	) John is <u>frustrating</u> me.) I am <u>deciding</u> whether or not to leave.) It is <u>satisfying</u> for me to change.
Nominalization	) There is <u>frustration</u> in my life.) The <u>decision</u> is made.) <u>Satisfaction</u> is part of change.

As can be seen from the examples, much information is automatically deleted when nominalizations are used.

Example:

Satisfaction is part of change.
) Satisfying for whom?
) What is satisfying?
deleted   ) Satisfying where?
) How is it satisfying?

Common Nominalizations

decision	anticipation
frustration	sensation
satisfaction	change
love	intuition
knowledge	perception
confusion	integration

Any of the aforementioned language patterns can be used in metaphor to enhance the effectiveness of the intervention. The patterns described can be used in a variety of ways and any number of them can be joined into a metaphor to elicit the desired outcome.

STACKING METAPHOR

A technique known as stacking metaphors is a useful way of creating depth in the story and thereby discouraging interference and interpretation by the conscious mind. Simply stated, stacking metaphors is the process of creating a metaphor within a metaphor. This stacking process can be done many times, thereby creating several levels of reality within the story. Each level of reality is created by developing for that level a context of its own.

Case Study

Client comes in and before there is even a chance to get acquainted, begins throwing out numerous words, jargon, labels and theories which might explain her problem. It seems that the jargon used was picked up by reading self-help books and from a previous therapist whom she had seen. In order to set the stage for a more experiential approach, not relying on the analysis which had failed for her before, the following metaphor was delivered:

You know, I had a thought come to mind. This reminds me of a client I once had who came in to solve a particular problem. I told her I would like to tell her a story that an old friend told me. My friend started that story by saying:

Once upon a time there was a rose bush, and on this rose bush grew the most beautiful rose in the whole world. This rose bush was located in a lush, green valley between two mountains and was the subject of many tales.

One day, a Zen master was passing through the area, and, having heard about the rose, went to see it. The Zen master, coming upon the rose, looked at it to see its beauty, sniffed its delicate fragrance and sat down next to the bush and meditated upon the rose. During the meditation the Zen master became one with the rose, and, after having felt that he understood its essence, he quietly continued along his journey.

A few months later, a scientist, also in search of understanding, came upon the rose. The first thing the scientist did was pluck a few petals, clip a few leaves, and cut off a piece of stem. Once these samples were secured in their own little plastic container, the scientist dug a soil sample and chopped off a piece of root. Finally, the scientist, unsatisfied with what he had taken in samples, dug up the remainder of the bush and carried it off.

This metaphoric presentation has four levels of reality. On one level, there is the client and the therapist. The second level is the therapist and the client he once had. Level three is the therapist and his friend, while the fourth and final level is the actual metaphor of the Zen master and the rose.

ELICITING STATES OF CONSCIOUSNESS

Metaphors are an extremely elegant way to elicit a response from a client. By using metaphors, a therapist can induce a particular state of consciousness, assist the client in gaining access to resources and/or create a context in which a particular problem would automatically be solved. The underlying presupposition of this technique is to find a context in which the desired outcome naturally occurs as a part of that experience. By delivering a metaphor, the therapist creates a context (an alternative reality) in which the client subjectively experiences the context and therefore gains access to the resource which lies within the parameters of the induced context.

A patient's brought to my office by ambulance. The patient had, possibly, three months more to live. And the patient was in very great pain, and drugs didn't seem to help at all. And she hadn't had drugs for more than eight hours when she arrived at my office. And she was wheeled in, and she said, "My doctor said you would use hypnosis to control my pain. And just the spoken word — that sounds ridiculous." I said, "Madam, just listen to me, and see if you can understand what I mean. As you sit there, if you saw a very hungry-looking tiger walk through that door into this room, and look at you and lick its chops, how much pain do you suppose you would feel?" She said, "I wouldn't feel any pain, I'd be thinking about the tiger. And now I notice I don't have any pain now, because I've gotten a new view of things." . . . And when she left, I asked her what she was going to do. And she said, "I'm going to have a good time, but I don't think the nurses will understand about the tiger that I'm going to keep under my bed. I don't think the doctor will understand, either." And everytime they ask her if she wanted drugs for her pain, she says "No, keeping the tiger there, anytime I need him."[37]

Metaphors are an extremely elegant tool, which when used in therapy can be both effective and creative. In many cases, the results of a delivered metaphor are not seen immediately because the metaphor needs time to incubate. By using metaphor, a therapist can gracefully work with a client in such a way as to assist him to gain access to his inherent potential.

Some fifteen or so years ago when the Denver zoo was going through a major renovation, there was a polar bear there, which had arrived at the zoo before a naturalistic environment was ready for it. Polar bears, by the way, are one of my favorite animals. They are very playful; they are big and graceful and do lots of nice things. The cage that it was put in temporarily was just big enough that the polar bear could take three nice, swinging steps in one direction, whirl up and around and come down and take three steps in the other direction, back and forth. The polar bear spent many, many months in that particular cage with those bars that restricted its behavior in that way. Eventually a naturalistic environment in which they could release the polar bear was built around this cage, on-site. When it was finally completed, the cage was removed from around the polar bear and to this very day the bear is still taking those three steps back and forth, in the same spot, even though the bars have been gone for years.[38]

FOOTNOTES

1. Nigel Calder, *Einstein's Universe*, p. 13.
2. A. Porter, *Cybernetics Simplified*, p. 37.
3. A. Korzybski, *Science and Sanity*, p. 58.
4. Richard Bandler, John Grinder, *The Structure of Magic*, p. 8.
5. *Ibid.*, pp. 8-13.
6. Robert Anton Wilson, *Cosmic Trigger*, p. XXIX.
7. Richard Bandler, John Grinder, *The Structure of Magic*, p. 14.
8. *Ibid.*, p. 15.
9. *Ibid.*, p. 16.
10. John Grinder, Richard Bandler, *The Structure of Magic,* Vol. II, pp. 6-9.
11. *Ibid.*, p. 9.
12. George Miller, "The Magic Number Seven, Plus or Minus Two: Some Limits On Our Capacity for Processing Information," *The Psychological Review*, Vol. 63, March, 1956.
13. Richard Bandler, John Grinder, *Frogs Into Princes*, p. 55.
14. Carlos Castaneda, *Journey To Ixtlan: The Lessons of Don Juan*, pp. 246-256.
15. Robert Dilts, John Grinder, Richard Bandler, Leslie C. Bandler, Judith Delozier, *Neuro-Linguistic Programming: Volume I*, pp. 76-82.
16. *Ibid.*
17. *Ibid.*
18. *Ibid.*
19. Leslie Cameron-Bandler, *They Lived Happily Ever After,* pp. 44-48.
20. Steve Lankton, *Practical Magic*, p. 59.
21. Ronald Wardhaugh, *Introduction to Linguistics*, pp. 207-220.
22. Leslie Cameron-Bandler, *They Lived Happily Ever After,* pp. 171-183.
23. Robert Dilts, John Grinder, Richard Bandler, Leslie C. Bandler and Judith Delozier, *Neuro-Linguistic Programming: Volume I*, p. 26.
24. Robert Dilts, *Neurolinguistic Programming: A New Psychotherapy,* (Unpublished Paper 1977), p. 16.
25. Leslie Cameron-Bandler, *They Lived Happily Ever After*, pp. 159-160.
26. Stan Woolams and Michael Brown, *T.A.: The Total Handbook Transactional Analysis*, p. 18.
27. Richard Bandler, John Grinder, *Frogs Into Princes*, pp. 83-87.
28. Leslie Cameron-Bandler, *They Lived Happily Ever After*, p. 115.
29. *Ibid.*, p. 117.
30. Paul Watzlawick, John Weakland, Richard Fisch, *Change*, p. 95.
31. Robert Dilts, *Neurolinguistic Programming: A New Psychotherapy,* (Unpublished Paper 1977), p. 20.
32. Steve Lankton, *Practical Magic*, pp. 114-115.

33. Leslie Cameron-Bandler, *They Lived Happily Ever After,* pp. 131-132.
34. Hyemeyohsts Storm, *Seven Arrows*, pp. 4-8.
35. Jay Haley, *Problem Solving Therapy*, pp. 66-67.
36. David Gordon, *Therapeutic Metaphor*, pp. 39-48.
37. Milton Erickson, *The Artistry of Milton Erickson, M.D., Part II,* p. 5.
38. Richard Bandler, John Grinder, *Frogs Into Princes*, p. 192.

BIBLIOGRAPHY

Bandler, Leslie Cameron, *They Lived Happily Ever After,* Cupertino, California: Meta Publication, 1978.

Bandler, Richard and Grinder, John, *Frogs Into Princes,* Moat, Utah: Real People Press, 1979.

Bandler, Richard and Grinder, John, *Patterns of The Hypnotic Techniques of Milton Erickson, M.D., Vol. I,* Cupertino, California: Meta Publications, 1975.

Bandler, R. and Grinder, J., *The Structure of Magic,* Palo Alto, California: Science and Behavior Books, Inc., 1975.

Calder, Nigel, *Einstein's Universe,* New York, New York: Penguin Books, 1980.

Castaneda, Carlos, *Journey To Ixtlan: The Lessons of Don Juan,* New York, New York: Simon & Schuster, 1972.

Dilts, Robert, *Neurolinguistic Programming: A New Psychotherapy,* "Unpublished Paper", 1977.

Dilts, Robert, Grinder, John, Bandler, Richard, Bandler, Leslie C. and Delozier, Judith, *Neuro-Linguistic Programming: Volume I,* Cupertino, California: Meta Publication, 1980.

Erickson, Milton, *The Artistry of Milton Erickson, M.D., Part II,* Haverford, Pennsylvania: Herbert S. Lustig, M.D., L.T.D., 1975.

Gordon, David, *Therapeutic Metaphors,* Cupertino, California: Meta Publications, 1978.

Grinder, J. and Bandler, R., *The Structure of Magic, Volume II,* Palo Alto, California: Science and Behavior Books, Inc., 1976.

Haley, Jay, *Problem Solving Therapy,* San Francisco, California: Josey-Bass Inc., 1976.

Korzybski, A., *Science and Sanity,* Lakeville, Connecticut: The International Non-Aristotelian Library Publishing Company, 4th Edition, 1933.

Lankton, Steve, *Practical Magic*, Cupertino, California: Meta Publication, 1980.

Miller, George, *The Magic Number Seven, Plus or Minus Two: Some Limits On Our Capacity for Processing Information*, "The Psychological Review", Vol. 63, March, 1956.

Porter, A., *Cybernetics Simplified*, New York, New York: Barnes and Noble, Inc., 1970.

Reps, Paul, *Zen Flesh, Zen Bones*, Garden City, New York: Doubleday & Company, Inc.

Storm, Hyemeyohsts, *Seven Arrows*, New York, New York: Harper and Row Publishers, Inc., 1972.

Wardhaugh, Ronald, *Introduction to Linguistics*, New York, New York: McGraw Hill, Inc., 1972.

Watzlawick, Paul, Weakland, John, and Fisch, Richard, *Change*, New York, New York: W.W. Norton and Company, Inc., 1975.

Wilson, Robert Anton, *Cosmic Trigger*, New York, New York: Pocket Books, 1977.

Woollams, Stan and Brown, Michael, *T.A.: The Total Handbook Transactional Analysis*, Englewood Cliffs, New Jersey: Prentice-Hall, Inc., 1979.

INDEX

TABLE OF ALGORITHMS

Metamorphous Press

METAMORPHOUS PRESS is a publisher and distributor of books and other media providing resources for personal growth and positive changes. MPI publishes and distributes leading edge ideas that help people strengthen their unique talents and discover that we all create our own realities.

Many of our titles have centered around NeuroLinguistic Programming (NLP). NLP is an exciting, practical and powerful model of human behavior and communication that has been able to connect observable patterns of behavior and communication to the processes that underlie them.

METAMORPHOUS PRESS provides selections in many subject areas such as communication, health and fitness, education, business and sales, therapy, selections for young persons, and other subjects of general and specific interest. Our products are available in fine bookstores around the world. Among our Distributors for North America are:

Baker & Taylor
Bookpeople
New Leaf Distributors
Pacific Pipeline

The Distributors
Inland Book Co.
Moving Books, Inc.

For those of you overseas, we are distributed by:
Airlift (UK, Western Europe)
Bewitched Books (Victoria, Australia)

New selections are added regularly and the availability and prices change so ask for a current catalog or to be put on our mailing list. If you have difficulty finding our products in your favorite store or if you prefer to order by mail we will be happy to make our books and other products available to you directly.

YOUR INVOLVEMENT WITH WHAT WE DO AND YOUR INTEREST IS ALWAYS WELCOME — please write to us at:

Metamorphous Press, Inc.
3249 N.W. 29th Avenue
P.O. Box 10616
Portland, Oregon 97210
(503) 228-4972

POSITIVE CHANGE GUIDE SERIES

Fitness Without Stress
A Guide to the Alexander Technique
Robert M. Rickover

Get The Results You Want
A Systematic Approach to NLP
Kim Kostere and Linda Malatesta

Magic of NLP Demystified
A Pragmatic Guide to Communication and Change
Byron Lewis and Frank Pucelik

The Power of Balance
A Rolfing View of Health
Brian W. Fahey, Ph.D.

NLP Series
from Metamorphous Press

SKILL BUILDER SERIES

The Excellence Principle
Scout Lee, Ed.D.
This standard in the field of NLP was originally a set of personal notes and formal thoughts. In its revised form, this workbook is packed with dynamic metaphors, ideas, exercises and visual aids.
1-55552-003-0 . . . paperback $16.95

Your Balancing Act
Carolyn Taylor
This NLP text presents systematic exercises and new material for changing the all important beliefs that underlie the conditions of wellness. Health, relationships, creativity and success are just a few aspects addressed.
0-943920-75-2 . . . paperback $12.95

Basic Techniques, Book I
Linnaea Marvell-Mell
This is the only NLP workbook available for those who wish to refine their NLP skills, people who have read books on the subject or attended seminars but want more. The book comes with a cassette tape. It complements the introductory book, *Magic of NLP Demystified* and reinforces NLP skills.
1-55552-016-2 . . . paperback $12.95

Advanced Techniques
Phill Boas with Jane Brooks
This manual is designed for use by those who have some knowledge of NLP. It is written from the perspective of the trainer/seminar leader, and much of the information is intended to help the group leader assist the participants to get maximum benefit from the 50 exercises.
0-943920-08-6 . . . paperback $ 9.95

Basic Techniques, Book II
Clifford Wright
This workbook provides additional tools to refine skills learned in *Basic Techniques, Book I*. Filled with exercises for individual practice or group work, *Basic Techniques II* provides ongoing skill-building in NLP technology
1-55552-005-7 . . . paperback $10.95

The Challenge of Excellence
Scout Lee, Ed.D.
Scout Lee's book is about utilizing challenge and playfulness to program the human computer for excellence. It has sophisticated information on body language and its connection to the mental process.
1-55552-004-9 . . . paperback $16.95